5 SPIRITUAL STEPS TO OVERCOME ADVERSITY

5 SPIRITUAL STEPS TO OVERCOME ADVERSITY

HOW TO USE THE COSMIC 2X4 TO HIT A HOMERUN

DR. JUDY MORLEY

Published 2021 by Gildan Media LLC
aka G&D Media
www.GandDmedia.com

FIRST EDITION 2021

Front cover design by David Rheinhardt of Pyrographx

Interior design by Meghan Day Healey of Story Horse, LLC

Library of Congress Cataloging-in-Publication Data is available upon request

ISBN: 978-1-7225-0562-2

10   9   8   7   6   5   4   3   2   1

Contents

Introduction

Congratulations. You've just been hit by a cosmic 2x4! I bet you never saw it coming. Although it probably doesn't feel like it, you've just been given a great gift. It is by overcoming challenging situations that we build our confidence, learn our resiliency, and deepen our appreciation for our abilities. You hold in your hands the secret to overcoming any challenge life can throw at you. Challenges open the doorway for you to express yourself fully, release old fears that have been holding you back, and go for the dreams you've been putting off. Once you realize that life's cosmic 2x4 is your ticket to happiness, you'll be able to turn it around and use it to hit a home run with your life! This book will show you how. I ask only that you approach it with an open mind and entertain the possibility that your current adversity was sent to actually *improve* your life. All the answers you seek are already inside you; you just need to access them.

First, you must define what success means to you. That may seem like an unrealistic activity, especially if you're mired in a serious challenge, but you can't take a step in any direction until you know where you're going. What does success look like? How does it feel? The journey from where you are now to where you want to be will provide the spiritual healing necessary to live the life of your dreams!

I have had multiple opportunities to overcome significant challenges, but perhaps the greatest came in 1998. I remember exactly where I was when I found out I had cancer. After six months of trying to figure out why I had a lump in my neck the size of a walnut, the doctors finally performed a biopsy in May of 1998. My family and I left on vacation the next day. Later that week from a hotel room in Cody, Wyoming, I called to get the test results. My three-year-old daughter and her father were swimming in the hotel pool, and I looked out at the majesty surrounding Yellowstone National Park while the doctor told me the news. I had Hodgkin's lymphoma. I was thirty-three years old.

That day started the greatest journey of my life. At first, it seemed like one shock after another. I returned from vacation, and we began the staging process. I figured that the cancer must be in the early stages, because the doctors had such a difficult time diagnosing it. I was wrong. I was in Stage 4, the final stage. I started a regimen of chemotherapy, only to learn that I was allergic to one of the drugs, and it burned my veins the entire three hours it dripped in. I had a mediport placed in my chest to mitigate the problem, but halfway through my six months of treatment I got a major bacterial infection in the port. The doctors decided to treat the infection with intravenous antibiotics, so I had a needle and tube in me, 24/7, for the last two months of my treatment. The mixture of chemo and antibiotics made me so sick that I almost landed back in the hospital because I couldn't stop vomiting. My white blood cells couldn't keep up, so I gave myself daily injections to build my immune system, just to have the chemo kill it again. I was sick, bald, scared, and fed up with doctors, nurses, hospitals, and anything that looked like medicine. On many occasions, it felt that it would be easier to die than continue the treatment.

Then, in my darkest hour, I had an epiphany. The answer to my problems didn't lie with the doctors, nurses, or drugs, but rather within me. I began to wonder, why do some people die and others live? What is the intangible element that causes some hopeless cases to fully recover, and other less severe patients to deteriorate in a matter of weeks? In a larger sense, I was asking the universal question: Why do bad things happen to good people? Then, it came to me. I realized I wasn't suffering because of the cancer as much as I was suffering from my own resistance to well-being. I decided that, regardless of the prognosis, I was going to live. There were so many things I still wanted to do! I wanted to see my toddler grow up, write a book, go to Europe, and have *fun* again. I began reading everything I could about cancer, medicine, the mind-body connection, non-traditional therapies, spirituality, and ongoing wellness.

All that reading taught me that people who allowed cancer to bring meaning to their lives survived longer and in greater numbers than those who gave up. I realized that I had been denying myself the things that mattered most to me, and consequently I'd sucked all the joy out of my life. My sickness was an outgrowth of my attitude. But I also learned that I had power—not only over my cancer, but over my life. Cancer wasn't about dying, but rather about changing the way I'd been living. That realization was the beginning of my healing.

In the years since I overcame cancer, I have recognized that all of life's curveballs serve the same purpose. They are the way that life tells us that we have strayed from the path of our highest good. The great mystical teacher Emma Curtis Hopkins claimed that God is Good, and said, "There is Good for me, and I ought to have it."* Every major religion teaches about a benevolent deity but frequently fails to extend that benevolence to humanity. The spiritual truth that transcends all dogma, however, is that God is Good, and wants us to have Good as well.

Often, we are taught differently, however. We learn we are unworthy and must prove ourselves before we can get our Good. However, if we are truly created in the image and likeness of God, as the Hebrew Scriptures claim, aren't we already worthy of perfect health, financial security, relational harmony, and career fulfillment? If no one tells us this when we are young, we frequently take the wrong path with our life and end up unfulfilled, unhappy, and unhealthy. How do we shift this? We have to begin making different choices. How do we know if we are not making choices that allow Good to come to us? We know because the universe sends us a challenge to help us examine and alter how we live. That challenge could be health-related, as mine was, or financial, relational, or career-based. Regardless of its origin, the adversity is really an opportunity.

You've probably already heard that adversity can be transformed into opportunity, but it's different when you're the one going through it. Accepting that it can be transformed, however, is foundational to all spiritual and emotional growth. All

---

* Emma Curtis Hopkins, *Scientific Christian Mental Practice* (Camarillo, CA: DeVorss, 1974), 17.

the great religious traditions teach us to learn from our challenges and use that information to create better experiences. When I talk about spiritual steps to success, I mean finding the way to live a life that is more fulfilling, more prosperous, more peaceful, and more inspiring than the life you've been living previously. There are plenty of ways to overcome adversity and thrive because of the experience. The point of this book is to help you do all of that while gaining a deeper understanding of life and all its facets. This understanding makes success a foregone conclusion in every area of your life.

In the following pages, I give you five simple steps to bring your body, mind, and spirit into alignment and find the power within you to create true success. The steps outlined in this book will give you the personal power to make informed choices. The information may seem very simple to you—it is, indeed, incredibly straightforward. There are no magic formulas, no complicated incantations, no strenuous exercises. Just five simple steps that will change your thinking, reframe your perspective, and bring you happiness and success for years to come. Be warned, however: these steps are simple, but they are not easy. Maintaining ongoing success means changing patterns of thought and behavior that you have had your whole life. It takes commitment, it takes courage, and it takes support, but I promise the results will be worth it.

Is Your Thinking Getting in Your Way?

If you are like most people who get smacked by a cosmic 2x4, you probably believe that you were victimized by an insidious enemy. From this perspective, you have no control over what has happened to you, and you probably feel angry, frustrated, helpless, and scared. You see events outside yourself as happening "to" you, and you are just the unsuspecting bystander who happened to get screwed. This way of thinking, which supposes that everything happens "out there," dates to philosopher René Descartes in the seventeenth century, and is the prevailing paradigm for all Western thought.

The problem with this paradigm, however, is that it takes control away from each of us. From this viewpoint, we are helpless against the enemy. We are completely disempowered to change our circumstances, since we had no control over their origins. Regardless of the situation, placing responsibility for adversity outside of ourselves leaves us feeling hopeless and helpless, emotions that actually increase vulnerability and susceptibility to poor choices.

Ever since the American Civil War a spiritual philosophy known as New Thought has suggested that we create our reality through our conscious and unconscious beliefs. So do the foundational, mystical traditions of all major religions, but those precepts sometimes get lost in religious dogma and are rarely part of their routine practice. According to New Thought, adversity is the universe reflecting back to us our hidden beliefs and giving us a chance to change them. Suppose for a minute that everything in your life has been attracted to you based on your attitudes and emotions. This may sound New Age, but really it is a very old philosophy. All of the ancient religions teach that there is a power greater than we are, and that we activate it through our conscious and unconscious thoughts. Jesus says in the Bible, "It is done unto you as you believe." In the past century, the field of quantum physics has supported the philosophical suggestions of New Thought, which I'll discuss a little later.

One of the most prominent New Thought teachers was a practical mystic named Ernest Holmes. Holmes claimed that there is a power greater than we are in the universe, and we can use it. He believed that this power worked according to a set of natural laws, similar to gravity, which we could harness, even if we didn't understand them. The way we harness those laws is through our thoughts. These laws work on *all* our thoughts—both conscious and unconscious. Many spiritual seekers can feel discouraged when they hear that, but this is where our power lies. If we can identify the unconscious beliefs that are no longer serving us, we can fix them at a deep level. By consciously creating a new thought (hence the name of the movement), we can create our lives anyway we want.

One of the most obvious places where New Thought has influence is in the mind/body connection. The principles of New Thought were identified in the era before modern medicine, so most of the early founders experienced miraculous physical healings by using the power of the mind. These well-documented cases provided hope for people who suffered physical ailments in the decades prior to the discovery of penicillin and other medical innovations. In the 1960s, Dr. O. Carl Simonton, a medical doctor, and his wife, Stephanie Matthews-Simonton, a psychologist, opened the Cancer Counseling and Research Center in Dallas, Texas.* They worked with patients who had been diagnosed as "medically incurable" and had

---

* For more information, see O. Carl Simonton, Stephanie Matthews-Simonton, and James L. Creighton, *Getting Well Again: A Step-by-Step, Self-Help Guide to Overcoming Cancer for Patients and Their Families* (New York: Bantam Books, 1978).

come to the Simontons' clinic as a last resort. Most had less than a year to live. The Simontons began using a technique they called "mental imagery" to help the so-called hopeless cases, and their results were astounding. Although almost 100 percent of their patients came to the clinic with less than one year to live, after four years by using the Simontons' technique, 68.4 percent of these people either had stabilized or were completely cured using nothing other than their minds.

I found this to be true in my own case. I had an unconscious belief that I could be loved only if I was perfect. I could never make a mistake. In the two years before I was diagnosed, I had tried to be super-mom and an outstanding graduate student and a perfect wife all at once. I was in a PhD program in another state, necessitating a commute of 450 miles each way, and yet I still carried straight As. I stacked all my courses into three days so that I would be away from home only on the days my toddler went to preschool. On my days off, I took my daughter to Gymboree, ballet, soccer, and swimming lessons. Weekends, my husband and I entertained like a perfect middle-class suburban couple. I was exhausted and miserable! But I was also deathly afraid to admit it—literally! I couldn't do it all, but admitting that meant losing my identity as the "perfect" wife, "perfect" mother, "perfect" student. I stayed on my self-created treadmill until cancer gave me a convenient excuse (ostensibly beyond my control) to get off without losing my "perfect" persona.

Dr. Lawrence LeShan, a psychotherapist who spent more than thirty-five years working with cancer patients, found evidence supporting the Simontons' research. According to LeShan, the psychological causes of cancer are frequently more compelling than the physical causes. He found that by facilitating psychological change in his patients, their physical survival rates increased. In addition, he discovered that when his clients failed to fulfill their life purpose, they compromised their immune system and got sick. LeShan's book, *Cancer as a Turning Point*, urged patients to use the experience of their illness as a way to refocus their lives. He showed that patients who learned important lessons from their cancer and changed the trajectory of their lives in accordance with those lessons went on to lead long, happy, and healthy lives.[*]

Our thoughts have a profound effect on the world around us, as well as on our own bodies. Our beliefs about the world create our expectations, which influence our attitudes, which impact our behavior. If we are fearful about money, the fear clouds our judgment and it is almost impossible to make wise business decisions. If we have no confidence, we will settle for a mate who doesn't value us. At the end of the day, our thoughts are the primary cause of all of experience—for better or worse.

The Role of Feelings

Feelings are a crucial part of the power of our thoughts. New Thought teaches that it is the thought *plus* the feeling that brings about the result. Yet the vast majority of us are taught to deny our feelings—both our emotions and our physical sensations. I remember the first time I had a headache. I was about nine years old and told my grandmother that I needed an aspirin. "You can't have a headache," she replied. "You're too young." Well, because I believed her, I denied headaches until I

---

[*] Lawrence LeShan, *Cancer as a Turning Point: A Handbook for People with Cancer, Their Families, and Health Professionals* (New York: Penguin Books, 1994), 74–76.

was eighteen years old, suffering through them in silence. Once I went to college, however, and allowed myself to take an aspirin, I quit having headaches altogether. It probably shouldn't have surprised me then that I denied my fatigue, low-grade fever, sore throat, and other lymphoma symptoms for almost eighteen months before the lump in my neck manifested. How could I possibly tune into what my body was feeling when I had spent almost thirty years perfecting the art of ignoring pain, fatigue, and illness?

Our emotions play a vital role in our success, but we frequently fail to recognize and honestly acknowledge them. Have you ever had a bad feeling in your gut about a situation, but you ignored it and went ahead anyway? Most people have experienced this, and it generally turns out badly. At the same time, we tend to deny ourselves those things that feel good, usually because we believe there's something else we're obligated to do. Do you forego a fun evening so you can do housework, or pay bills instead of doing something creative, or check your work e-mail in the evenings rather than read a novel? It is important to keep up on our responsibilities, of course, but when we ignore or override our feelings, we actually block the good that is trying to come into our lives. It is our attitude toward what we are doing and toward the have-to items that we pack into our schedules that creates stress. *Stress* is a catchall term for many things, including anger, fear, resentment, anxiety, and depression. Can you recognize when you have stress in your life? Can you distinguish the more subtle feelings underneath it? Do you know which emotion is actually driving the stress—anger, fear, or anxiety? Identifying and managing our feelings are keys to successful living.

When I was young, my parents and role models taught me that as long as everything looked okay from the outside, it didn't matter how I felt on the inside. If I was upset, I was told to cheer up so that I wouldn't make the people around me uncomfortable. I'm sure I'm not the only person who was raised this way.

Somewhere along the line, our culture began to misconstrue the display of emotion as a sign of weakness. This especially pertains to men, but even women are taught that we get too old to cry, that anger isn't appropriate, that there's nothing to be afraid of, and that we should always put on a happy face. These platitudes do an incredible disservice to our success. By keeping emotions bottled up, we add to the daily stress in our lives, and the fact that we have been trained to ignore these signals leaves us in a powder-keg situation, where stress builds with no productive outlet until it has to erupt somewhere.

The adversity life brings us, then, is a way to get our attention and force us to deal with our emotions. Many people who've lost lucrative jobs have said in the long run that it's the best thing that ever happened to them. People facing divorce may feel it's the end of the world, but five years later report that the end of that relationship paved the way for them to find the mate of their dreams. Many cancer survivors claim that, although their time going through cancer was difficult, it was one of the greatest gifts of their life. By grieving for an old situation, we're forced to face feelings and emotions that have been smoldering under the surface, sometimes for decades.

Feelings don't exist in a vacuum—our feelings are dictated by our thoughts. In any given situation, we choose to interpret events a certain way (thoughts), which then dictates our attitude about them (feelings). For example, if a salesperson in a department store is rude to me, either I can view it as a personal insult, which will lead me to be angry and frustrated, or I can choose to believe that the person is having a bad day, let it go, and find someone else to help me. That's a fairly simple example, but it shows that we have a choice in how we feel. Because thoughts dictate feelings, they play a crucial role in our emotional and physical health.

The Good News: You Can Control Your Thoughts

Instead of thinking of yourself as victimized by some external force, why not accept the possibility that your own thoughts are the root cause of whatever situation you're facing? More specifically, the ingrained beliefs that you've accepted as the truth are causing trouble, and your current circumstances are telling you to get back in alignment. That, of course, means that you can change your thoughts and, consequently, your situation. Change can be a terrifying thing, however. Most of us retreat to what is comfortable, even if it costs us dearly. As the phrase tells us, "Better the devil you know than the devil you don't." By facing the unknown devil, however, and changing your thoughts, you can ensure a reversal in your fortunes and enjoy a long and healthy life.

What thoughts are holding you back? The hardest part about answering that question is that most of us aren't aware of our deepest, most ingrained thoughts, so we don't know which ones are blocking us and which are moving us forward. How can we tell? By the way they make us feel. Because our thoughts send out energetic frequencies that attract experiences, perceptions, and situations to us, the way these thoughts make us feel tells us if we're moving closer to the things we want. It's practically impossible to monitor our thinking all the time, but our feelings tell us if our thoughts are attracting positive experiences or negative ones. Tuning into our feelings helps us get a sense of which thoughts serve us and which do not.*

Even after years of therapy, some people still don't have access to the deep, subconscious ideas they've carried with them since childhood. Most of the time, that's not a problem—those beliefs make us who we are, and we accept them with tacit resignation. When we're faced with an immediate challenge, however, we have an urgent reason to examine these thought patterns. It's like cleaning out the attic: you find a few things worth keeping and many worth discarding. Like old photos and outdated clothes, some items make you feel embarrassed, ashamed, and regretful, whereas others evoke joy and appreciation. Hitting a home run with the cosmic 2x4 is like cleaning out the attic. It's time to get rid of those thoughts that don't make you feel good.

Feeling good is the whole point of life. Whether you were raised Christian, Jewish, Hindu, Muslim, quantum scientist, or atheist, you must accept that there is *something*—an energy, a power, a force field—that holds the universe together, and it is from this field that everything was created. This energy is positive well-being, and when you're in alignment with it, you feel good! You don't have to believe in the scary man in the

---

* Jerry and Esther Hicks, *Ask and It Is Given: Learning to Manifest Your Desires* (Carlsbad, CA: Hay House, 2004).

clouds throwing lightning bolts, but you do have to believe in an energy, knowledge, and power greater than your current human understanding.

Mystics throughout the ages have taught that the higher power created humans to experience and express joy. You are supposed to feel good. Many of us were brought up to believe that feeling good is sinful, lazy, or somehow unspiritual. On the contrary, the infinite source did not bring the earth into physical form to make us all suffer. So get it through your head RIGHT NOW that you are supposed to feel good. That doesn't mean that you're supposed to feel good only after you have your health in order, or when you get a certain amount of money in savings, or after the kids are grown, or once your work's complete, your novel's written, your degree's finished, or your son's married. You're supposed to enjoy your life right now. *Right now.* So clean out your attic of any thoughts that don't make you feel good.

The Law of Attraction

In the past ten years, many people who study the field of personal development have heard about the Law of Attraction,* which is a spiritual law that explains how we create our experience. Every thought has a frequency that can be measured by using sophisticated brain-mapping and biofeedback technology. When you think a thought, it emits a frequency, attracting thoughts and experiences that vibrate at that same frequency. If you think positive, successful thoughts, you attract positive,

---

* See, for example, Rhonda Byrne, *The Secret* (New York: Atria Books, 2006).

successful experiences. Conversely, if you think toxic, negative thoughts, you attract toxic, negative experiences.*

The Law of Attraction has been substantiated by years of research in the field of quantum physics. I know you saw those words, quantum physics, and your eyes glazed over. Stick with me here. Quantum physics is the science behind creation, and aren't we really talking about creating a different reality? I want you to know that it is possible to create whatever reality you choose, and quantum physics is the science that allows you to do that. So take a deep breath, open your mind, and read on.

Quantum physics is the name scientists use to describe the study of subatomic particles too small to see with a microscope. It is a massively complex field with multiple theories and implications, and is far beyond my comprehension and the scope of this book. However, a basic explanation of it helps us understand the Law of Attraction by proving that thoughts create the physical world.

For more than a century, quantum physicists have observed that subatomic particles have the potential to take any form, and the form they ultimately take is dictated by the perspective of the observer. For example, matter can be in multiple places at any given time. It is only when someone observes it that it's fixed into a certain time and place. That means that all possible outcomes exist simultaneously.

---

* For more information on the Law of Attraction, see Jerry and Esther Hicks, *The Law of Attraction* (Carlsbad, CA: Hay House, 2004); Wayne Dyer, *You'll See It When You Believe It* (New York: Avon Books, 1989); Joe Vitale, *The Attractor Factor: 5 Easy Steps for Creating Wealth (or Anything Else) from the Inside Out* (Hoboken, NJ: Wiley and Sons, 2005); Jack Canfield, *The Success Principles: How to Get from Where You Are to Where You Want to Be* (New York: Harper Collins, 2006); Denis Waitley, *The Psychology of Winning* (New York: Berkley Books, 1986).

Think about that last sentence! *ALL possible outcomes exist simultaneously.* Pretty deep stuff, I know, and I can't begin to do it justice, but there are many wonderful books on the topic that can explain it.* For example, if you've been diagnosed with a serious illness, this means simply that the healthy you and the sick you are both here, RIGHT NOW, and the one you're experiencing is dictated by your expectations. If you expect sickness, you get more of it. If you expect wellness, you get that.

You may say, but I'm a positive person! How can I have possibly attracted a cosmic 2x4? Good question. Most people hate to hear the answer. The Law of Attraction is impeccable—it works the same way, every time, for every person, no exceptions. It responds to your predominant vibration, the entire body of your thoughts and emotions, conscious and subconscious. A piece of conventional wisdom that's widely quoted by self-help gurus and New Thought teachers is, "We don't attract what we *want*; we attract what we *are*." You may be consciously talking yourself into thinking positive thoughts, but if they are only a mask covering negative, unhealthy, stressful thoughts buried in your subconscious, your positive and negative frequencies are canceling each other out. This doesn't mean that the situation you're facing is your fault. It does mean that the challenge is giving you an opportunity to identify your negative thought patterns.

Now you might be asking, how can I control my subconscious thoughts? After all, they're *subconscious*! That's where

---

* For a straightforward discussion of quantum physics, see Fred Alan Wolf, *The Spiritual Universe: How Quantum Physics Proves the Existence of the Soul* (New York: Simon and Schuster, 1996); Wolf, *Mind into Matter: A New Alchemy of Science and Spirit* (Needham, MA: Moment Point Press, 2000); Amit Goswami, *Physics of the Soul: The Quantum Book of Living, Dying, Reincarnation and Immortality* (Charlottesville, VA: Hampton Roads Publishing, 2001); Alistair I. M. Rae, *Quantum Physics: A Beginner's Guide* (Oxford: One World Publications, 2006).

the Law of Attraction can help. We attract whatever is like our most prevalent vibrations. Most of us spend the majority of our time thinking about what we do not want. We get caught up in worry, fear, and anxiety and lose sight of those things we want to attract. We give up hope that things can change for us, so we continue to attract more of what we already have and do not want. However, if we keep our minds focused on those things we do want, we attract those. In the words of the most famous quantum physicist, Albert Einstein, "We cannot solve our problems with the same thinking we used when we created them."

Research on mind-body wellness and peak performance supports the Law of Attraction. In the case of the Simontons' work with cancer patients, they found that people who did daily guided meditations survived more frequently. The guided meditations focused their patients' attention on the desired outcome. The Simontons encouraged their patients to visualize their own immune systems as powerful warriors slaying the cancer cells, or as a powerful chemical that dissolved the invaders. Personally, I visualized my white blood cells as little Pac Men® traveling through the corridors of my bloodstream, munching up any cell that didn't belong there. This powerful technique *attracted* that very situation. Visualization creates healing because it focuses attention on wellness. This is also true of Olympic athletes, Wall Street tycoons, and movie stars. You'll hear about several such success stories later in this book.

This means that, although you are scared and anxious about whatever is happening in your life, you must keep your mind focused on the outcome you *want*. Easier said than done, I know. It's hard to be focused on the magnificence of your life when there's a glitch in the system. It's hard to feel gratitude for your blessings when you're feeling like you've been attacked by the enemy. It's hard to have faith in a positive outcome when everything you've been taught by your family, your culture, and the media tells you that you're in deep trouble—but you must do it. You simply must. This book will show you how.

Still afraid you can't do it? Let me tell you about a young man from Upstate New York. He was raised in a wealthy, patrician family on an estate overlooking the Hudson River. After college, he decided to go into politics—a decision that mortified his family, since the rough-and-tumble world of public service was seen to be beneath him. Nevertheless, he was elected to the state senate and the US Senate, became the assistant secretary to the Navy, and ran for vice president in 1920. You may know, by now, that I'm talking about Franklin D. Roosevelt. Most people know that he went on to become the president of the United States, but not as many know about the cosmic 2x4 that hit him at what seemed to be the height of his political career.

Although he was not elected in 1920, his political star was still on the rise. Then, in 1921, he contracted polio. In the 1920s, polio was a death sentence, and those who did survive were permanently paralyzed. Roosevelt refused to believe that this was his destiny, however, and spent five years in physical therapy, some of that time in an iron lung, to overcome the disease. He survived, but all the pundits were certain that this was the end of his political career. Attitudes about people with physical challenges weren't nearly as progressive in the 1920s as they are today, and it was just about impossible for someone who needed a wheelchair to go any further in politics.

Roosevelt refused to believe the naysayers. He continued his physical therapy and solicited the help of engineers to create devices to help him walk normally, even if just for short distances. He innovated a podium with built-in leg braces so that he could appear to be standing behind it without assistance. He requested that the media not photograph him in his wheelchair, and they obliged. He figured out a way to hold on to the arms of his advisers so that it appeared he was walking on his own, while actually using them for support. All of this led him to re-enter public life, run for president, and get elected to an unprecedented four terms.

Roosevelt didn't succeed *despite* the adversity he faced; he succeeded *because* of it. When he ran for president in 1932, the United States was in the depth of the Great Depression. The other candidates, both in his party and others, counseled patience while the government and private sectors implemented rational, tried-and-true, economic strategies. Roosevelt, however, had learned to empathize with people who were struggling. Despite his background of wealth and privilege, he recognized that people needed to know that their leader understood adversity and had an idea about overcoming it. Like his own refusal to believe in his paralysis, he refused to believe that the economy would regulate itself and wanted the people to know that he would do whatever it took to improve their situations. He said, when running for election in 1932, "Once I spent two years in bed trying to move my big toe. After that everything else seems easy."

The insight and empathy FDR gained from his battle with polio gave him the wherewithal to fight for a higher ideal, create new economic systems to provide a social safety net, and ultimately bring the United States out of the Depression. Historians still debate whether Roosevelt's programs actually accomplished what he believed they would, but it was his willingness to try anything, *absolutely anything*, to help the American public that allowed people to keep faith in him and in democratic capitalism. He is rightly considered one of the most influential presidents in US history, and he could not have done any of it if it hadn't been for the great gift of polio.

I know this is a lot to absorb, especially if you're new to thinking about thoughts as things and struggles as gifts. That's okay—you have every right to be a little skeptical. Whether or not you believe in spirituality, whether or not you're familiar with the science behind it, the steps in this book will work for you if you are willing to approach them with an open mind and a willingness to try anything. If you do that, you will experience a healing that will restore your body and affairs, as well as change your outlook on life and have you telling your friends ten years from now, as I do, that this cosmic 2x4 was the greatest gift you've ever experienced.

A Five-Step Process

In this book I offer you a five-step process to release the negative emotions and replace them with thoughts that promote your ongoing success. This book will show you how to get in touch with your feelings, both physical and emotional, and let go of the baggage that has weighed you down. All you have to do is be open to change.

Again, the steps may sound simple, but they aren't easy. They ask you to step outside your comfort zones and examine deeply buried, painful thoughts. It will take courage to go through the steps, and changing a lifetime of negative thoughts won't happen overnight. I frequently tell people that I was cured of cancer in 1998, but I'm still healing from it. Since that time, I have used these steps to get through financial challenges, the end of relationships, and career transitions, and I always find a new level of emotional healing. If you follow the steps in this book, you'll discover strength, health, and joy you never even dreamed possible. I promise.

In the subsequent chapters, I outline every step in detail, giving you the ideology and science behind each concept, telling you why it's important, and then providing concrete activities to work through the process. The best way to use this book is to read it through once quickly, then go back and take your time with each section. Do the worksheets at the end of the chapters, and focus on the feelings that come up for you. If you find yourself wanting to avoid a section, that is a signal that you need *that* information more than any other. We tend to avoid those things that are the most painful, but it is highly likely that the pain is an indicator that those are the specific toxic emotions that you need to release. When you get the feeling you don't want to continue a section, take a deep breath, visualize yourself safely completing the worksheet, and move forward.

Don't procrastinate on the uncomfortable chapters! It may not be comfortable or fun, but it's better than repeating this life lesson over and over. Staying comfortable has contributed to your current situation. You are taking an emotional risk by facing your fears, but you must do it in order to live the life you want. Know that you are safe. In the privacy of your own mind, things can hurt you only if you let them. It's time to let go of the events, circumstances, and memories that are causing you emotional pain, discomfort, and physical illness. Look at them head on, diffuse their power over you, and release them. The worksheets at the end of each chapter will help you through the process. Each chapter also includes a guided meditation. If you've never meditated before, it's a practice I highly recommend, and here's why. We are deluged with thoughts every day about a lot of different things. Most of these thoughts are negative—we worry about money, the future, our relationships, our job, and our health. We concoct all sorts of different scenarios, and they usually aren't good. We rarely fantasize about getting the stuff we want, like signing a big deal, being our ideal weight, or having perfect health. Instead, we see ourselves in dire circumstances and worry ourselves sick, literally, trying to deal with situations that will never occur.

Meditation is a wonderful way to stop all of this worrying and negative self-talk. Meditation is merely the process of quieting your mind. Our thoughts are like a constant background recording. Although we can tune it out at times, it gets increasingly annoying. If we shut off the recording, we enjoy the silence. This is how meditation works. It allows you to shut off the noise and negative messages your mind is sending, and it gives you a respite from the agitation. Author Marianne Williamson likens meditation to soaking dirty pans. Sometimes we have gunk solidly stuck to us, but soaking for a while will loosen it up and let it easily wash away.*

---

* Marianne Williamson, *The Gift of Change: Spiritual Guidance for Living Your Best Life* (San Francisco: HarperSanFrancisco, 2006).

The Simontons found meditation to be a crucial factor in the recovery of their clients. In fact, a large portion of the treatment they gave their patients was based on guided meditation and mental imagery. Meditation has repeatedly been proven to mitigate physical illnesses, everything from heart disease and high blood pressure to strokes and cancer. It can't hurt to try it, and it will certainly help.

Many people will say, "But I don't know how to meditate!" This is a tough comment to address, because there really is no right or wrong way. As long as you put your brain on pause, you are meditating. Some people say they can meditate while in the car at a stoplight; others have to set aside hours in a dark and quiet room. I recommend taking just a few minutes and focusing on your breathing—clearing your mind of any thought except your breath flowing in and out of your lungs. Set a timer for five minutes, and as you quiet your mind, you'll feel aligned with the beauty, joy, and power of the universe. The power is in the stillness.

Don't worry about getting it right. The meditations at the end of each chapter will guide you through the process. It's just important that you meditate. You must begin to train your mind to focus on wellness, empowerment, peace, love, and success, rather than enduring the constant worry and chatter that come from leaving the mind's tape player running without supervision. You'll feel energized by meditation and ready to tackle each new step.

Step 1 asks you to *Make Peace with Where You Are*. This step helps you face your fear and anger, and gives you exercises to identify and gain control over your emotions. The biggest component of the first step is forgiveness. Forgiveness is a powerful practice that facilitates the release of negative emotions and empowers you to move forward, free of the weight you've been carrying. Many people are reluctant to forgive because they feel that they are either condoning another person's bad behavior, or admitting that the other person was right. In the first step, I explain that this is not the case. Carrying your anger around isn't hurting the other person—it's hurting you. We will also talk about gratitude and its powerful properties. Finally, we will cover accepting your current situation openly and honestly, without any accompanying fear and anger.

In Step 2, I show you how to *Take Responsibility* for your situation. This gives most people pause, especially those who feel victimized. "How on earth am I responsible for this?" they ask. The answer takes some open-minded thinking and a deeper understanding of the Law of Attraction, which we will go into in detail in this chapter. However, responsibility is not the same as blame. Blame suggests that you did something wrong. Your current challenge is a situation that happened to you— not right or wrong, good or bad. It is giving you feedback about your life's path. By taking responsibility, you are empowering yourself to change the situation. Think of it as a compound of the words "response" and "ability." You have the ability to positively respond to this situation and to change it so that you like the outcome. If we had no responsibility for the situation, we would have no power to change it. By knowing we are response-able, we feel confident that we can create a different future.

Step 3 will *Identify the Benefits* of the situation. Whatever has happened to you is the path of least resistance. This may seem radical at first, but we live in a universe that works without effort. You are facing whatever challenge because that has become easier than taking the steps to do it differently. In my case, I was running myself ragged trying to be the perfect mother, perfect wife, perfect daughter, and perfect student. I was mortified at the idea that I might fail at any of those tasks. I refused to ask for help because I saw that as a form of failure, so I just kept on the treadmill, getting more and more unhappy, fearful, and stressed. This was easier than facing decades' worth of fear and insecurity that operated below my level of awareness. Cancer gave me an excuse to rest—doctor's orders. I didn't consciously think this way, but after years of examining the situation, I now can clearly see that getting sick was the path of least resistance. It gave me a way out of the situation and allowed me to stop being perfect for a while. It also provided me a way to release the resistance to other paths. Step 3 will help you identify how your current situation is providing the path of least resistance in your life.

Step 4 teaches you to *Release Limiting Beliefs*. We're brought up with a lot of ideas about the way the world works. Some of these ideas are valuable, like, "Eat your vegetables to grow up big and strong," "You need your beauty sleep," and "A penny saved is a penny earned." Many of the ideas we hear as children do not serve us, however. In their desire to protect us, our parents may have counseled us to abandon our dreams, squelch our creativity, and suppress our talent in order to be "practical." As we age, our hearts cry out to reconnect with those dreams. The stress that comes from abandoning those dreams and living a limited life is the kind of stress that contributes to disease, fosters relationship issues, and creates financial limitation. Step 4 will help you release the beliefs that have limited you.

Finally, Step 5 will help you *Make a Plan for Ongoing Success.* This is where the rubber hits the road. You've made peace with yourself, taken responsibility for your situation, identified the benefits it's bringing you, released any limiting beliefs, and now it's time to take action. This step shows you how to move in the direction of your desires and gives you specific action items. As the old saying goes, no one plans to fail—they just fail to plan. This step will ensure you have a plan. The underlying idea is that truly happy people have a life that works. This may be hard to swallow at first. I'm making the distinction between people who are making the best of their situation, and people who are truly living their life on purpose, connected to their source, following their dreams every day, and existing in a constant state of joy. Because of my health challenge, I know for sure that when we are in a state of joy, cancer cells can't live in our body. The biochemistry won't allow it. The meditation and worksheets in this chapter will help you define your life's purpose, give you ideas about how to make it possible, and show you how to choose joy in everything you do.

One thing that may help you make a plan for lifelong success is to hire a coach. Olympic athletes, professional football teams, and corporate executives understand the value of having coaches to keep them focused, help them resist falling back into bad habits, and achieve their highest potential. If you want to overcome your current condition and keep yourself focused on the life of your dreams, it will probably serve you to hire one. There are professional coaches out there at every price range, with many areas of specialization.

In just a few paragraphs, you'll find the first guided meditation in this book. I suggest that you read it through to yourself, then read it slowly into a recorder so that you can play it back. If that doesn't work, ask a spouse, family member, or trusted friend to read it slowly for you so that you can get into a state of meditation. Remember, you don't have to do it perfectly—just give it a try, focus on your breath, still your mind, and relax. If that's all you are able to do the first time, that's accomplishing a lot.

I know that you can do this. People overcome adversity in an instant when they change their beliefs. Stories of spontaneous healing appear frequently, and these stories all have one thing in common—the person stopped living in a state of fear and worry and started enjoying life. Deepak Chopra tells a story of a young woman diagnosed with non-Hodgkin's lymphoma, in the last stage. She sought treatment from the finest hospital in the Northeast and underwent multiple rounds of chemotherapy and radiation. Both her parents were physicians and pressured her to continue the traditional course of treatment, which wasn't working. Finally, to escape the pressure, she left the country to follow her dream of living in a small European town for a year. She took the Simontons' book, *Getting Well Again*, with her. A year later, she returned to Boston with no evidence of disease, completely puzzling her doctors. She lived her dream and "thought" herself well.*

You are a manifestation of the great Source. You were put on this earth to thrive. Life is meant to be a stream of pure, positive energy. The only reason you are not experiencing everything you desire is that you have done something to pinch off this flow. But you can get back into it. All it takes is let-

---

* Deepak Chopra, *Creating Health* (Boston: Houghton Mifflin, 1997), 23–24.

ting go, releasing your old ideas, and moving forward to ease, joy, emotional well-being, and health. Decide to feel healthy, loved, and prosperous, right here and now, regardless of the current situation, and it will all come to you.

So, are you ready to start the journey?

Meditation—Power and Healing

Get into a comfortable position, either sitting in a chair, on the floor, or lying down. Take a moment or two to fidget if you need to, as long as you get comfortable. Once you've found a position that suits you, begin to focus on your breathing. Feel yourself inhaling and exhaling, and notice the transition between the two—inhaling and exhaling. As you exhale, release the tension in your muscles and feel your whole body get heavy and relaxed. Clear your mind of all thoughts. If a thought comes into your head, bless it and then imagine you are exhaling that thought into a helium balloon. When you complete the exhale, let go of the balloon in your mind, and allow it to gently float away, clearing your mind again.

(Pause)

Once your mind is still, imagine that you are walking through a beautiful forest. The sun filters through the canopy of trees, and the day is warm and calm. Imagine that you can hear birds chirping, insects buzzing, and a gentle breeze rustling through the trees. Really put yourself into the scene. It may be a place you've been before, or it may be somewhere wholly imagined. Take some time to set the stage for your walk in the forest.

(Pause)

As you feel the forest all around you, look up and find the tallest, widest, sturdiest tree. It should be nearby, close at hand. Walk over to the tree, giving thanks for the beauty that surrounds it and the peaceful setting that it oversees. Now imagine that you are touching the tree. Feel the texture of the bark, the grooves along the trunk, the temperature of the surface. Lean against the tree, allowing it to hold most of your weight. Take a few minutes to breathe into the feeling of passing the weight of your worries on to the tree.

(Pause)

As you imagine yourself leaning against the tree, feel yourself soaking up the tree's strength. This tree has withstood decades, perhaps centuries, of wind, rain, lightning, snowfall, and sunshine. Its trunk is scarred and grooved, but each imperfection represents a place of healing—a place where the tree's bark grew back stronger than before. Feel yourself absorbing that strength.

(Pause)

Now see your body strong, like the trunk of the tree. Through your breath, feel yourself aligned with the entire universe—the sunshine, the clouds, the grasses, the tree, the insects, the wildlife, the forest. Know that you are connected to each and every living thing you've imagined in the forest, and everything that exists right here, right now, on the planet. Focus on the power that comes from the feeling of connectedness to the natural world. Feel the strength that radiates from the massive trunk of the tree against which you're leaning. Take some more deep breaths, and with each one, breathe in the power of connection. Imagine the cells of your body puffing up with every breath. Know that you are supported by the tree, and beyond that, by all the power available in the universe.

(Pause)

Now, silently thank the tree for its strength and support. Observe the forest once again, and thank the surroundings for being part of the energy that cleanses and empowers your body. As you turn to walk away from the tree, feel a new sense of empowerment. Take your steps deliberately as you walk to the edge of the forest. Breathe more deeply, and hold your head a little higher. Throw your shoulders back and walk with purpose. As you imagine yourself leaving the forest, you notice a glowing, clear path heading off to the horizon. The path climbs a slight hill, but you know that you are now strengthened; you are now prepared to walk on this path. This is the path to wellness. Picture yourself moving along the trail with optimism, joy, and power.

(Pause)

When you have deeply ingrained the sense of power in your subconscious, take another deep breath, and slowly bring your awareness back to the room.

Make Peace with Where You Are

Whatever you resist, persists.
—CARL JUNG

Welcome to the first of the Five Spiritual Steps to Success. In this step you'll learn the importance of accepting where you are right now. Remember the discussion about quantum physics and the Law of Attraction? These scientific paradigms tell us that we attract the object of our focus. If you are angry, fearful, and resentful about whatever situation you are facing, you are focusing on what you *don't* want—and that is a surefire way to attract more of it into your life. You must *make peace with where you are* so that you can focus on what you want, which is vibrant success.

Facing Fear

The first hurdle you must overcome is fear. Adversity is a way of showing you the result of carrying fear you've had your entire life—fear of failure, fear of rejection, and fear of criticism, among others—so it's understandable that this is your first reaction. Your current situation is really just a manifestation of all those fears that have built up over the years and pinched off your stream of well-being. That's why, in order to make peace with where you are, you MUST face your fears—all of them. It means facing the fears you've spent your lifetime avoiding. These include fears that you may still carry from childhood. Many of these are buried deep in your subconscious. After all, you've worked long and hard to suppress them. In order to heal, you must now dig them up and face them, but before you can face them, you first have to identify them.

Let's start with the fear that is right in front of your face. What fear does the current adversity amplify? What is it that takes your breath away? Taken to its most extreme outcome, what do you fear will happen? Regardless of your situation, I'm sure bad news is everywhere. If you're struggling with a rela-tionship challenge, I'm sure you're inundated with statistics about how hard it is to find a date, or perhaps with the high divorce rates in the nation, or the most sensational celebrity break-up. If you're worried about finances, you can always find dire news about the economy. If it's a health issue you face, perhaps the TV ads for new medications are capturing your attention. It's as if you can't get away from information that seems to validate and feed your fears!

Most of the fears stem from a significant fear for the future. What if this adversity hinders your life plans? What if you don't survive it? You can't help but have these thoughts, and they all evoke fear and worry, but I'm going to tell you something rad-ical. Those of you who are ready to hear this, will, but I hope you'll have an open mind. Adversity is *meant* to change your future. Let me say that again, a slightly different way. The reason you are experiencing this challenge is that your life was going down a path that wasn't working for you. This event is a signal to get back on track! Try to release the fear for the future. If you take the steps in this book, your future will be better than you could have possibly planned it.

In addition to these immediate fears, there are also hidden fears. These are the hardest to deal with, because you've had them a long time and they're second nature to you. You probably don't consciously recognize how often you think fearful thoughts each day, because they've become a habit, like brushing your teeth or driving to work. In this step, you will learn to uncover these fears and do whatever it takes to resolve them.

How do you face fears you don't even know you have? One way is to tune into your body's signals. We are born with a vast array of wonderful emotions, but by the time we start school, most of us have forgotten how to feel them. We are told *not* to cry, *not* to be afraid, to cheer up, to be nice when we don't want to be nice, and to deny any negative emotion we have. But our emotions are very real, however, and they must find a release. One way they do that is physical—headaches, backaches, nausea, and yes, cancer. Each emotion has a different physical manifestation.* These emotions also manifest in inappropriate behaviors such as addictions, and a lack of clarity about what we want, which causes us to put up with situations that don't work for us and then rationalize the outcome.

_____

* For more on the role of emotions on your health, see Louise Hay, *You Can Heal Your Life*, (Carlsbad, CA: Hay House, 1999).

I'm not telling you anything you don't already know. Most of us accept that our bodies are indicators of our fears, and we are all familiar with the frequent accuracy of a gut feeling. If you've ever had a tension headache or gotten a cold after a week of working long hours or had sore shoulders or lower back pain, you know that your emotions affect your health. To get rid of the condition, you must listen to your body's clues and figure out what they are trying to tell you. How do you do this? You practice. Every morning when you wake up, do a mental scan of your body to find out how it feels. Identify areas where your muscles feel tight, where you have pain, or where you feel like something isn't working quite right. Once you've done that, close your eyes and ask your body what feeling is causing the physical sensation. I promise that you will get an answer every single time. It will take some practice to recognize the message, and you must be willing to listen. Unfortunately, most people don't want to hear that anything is wrong, so they filter out their intuition. Stay open, keep at it, and you will get your answer.

The next step is asking how you habitually respond to that feeling. Do you overreact? Drink too much? Go shopping for things you can't afford? Pick a fight with your partner? Facing our fears means not only learning to recognize them, but also identifying the unsupportive patterns we use to suppress them.

Facing your fears takes some level of faith. Regardless of your religious beliefs, or lack thereof, you will have an easier time handling the fear if you don't try to face it alone. Believing in a benevolent universe does no harm and can help you feel a greater sense of peace and well-being as you move forward in this journey. If you don't have any religious or spiritual habits, now is a great time to consider embracing some. If you are absolutely opposed to the idea of acknowledging a higher power, then see a therapist or find a trusted friend or relative who can support you as you face your fears. It is always easier to feel unafraid when you share the experience with someone. Going it alone can be tough.

Following is a short meditation that will give you some techniques to identify and confront your deepest fears. You may do this anytime you feel discomfort in your body or have a conscious sensation of fear. Do it repeatedly and you'll find yourself uncovering and releasing more fear every time.

Short Meditation

Get into a comfortable position, either sitting or lying down. Take a deep breath, and feel your body completely relax. Let go of the muscles in your face, your neck, your shoulders, your back, your arms, and your legs.

(Pause)

Now, in your mind, go to a place you remember from childhood as being fun, safe, warm, and loving. It may be a place in your home, or a favorite neighborhood play spot, a tree fort, or a friend's home. The important thing is that you have wonderful memories of this spot, and you feel safe there. If there's really no place like that from your memory, use your imagination to create one. Get into the feeling of being there, right now, and allow whatever positive feelings you have to well up.

(Pause)

Now, see yourself as a child, as if your younger self were there with you right now. Greet your younger self, and assure him or her that it is completely safe. Now, ask your younger self how he or she feels. Ask him/her to tell you about any fear or anger that s/he is harboring about anything, toward anyone. Listen carefully. If the child is angry, remember that the anger is covering fear. Some of these fears will feel and sound familiar to you. Listen to the child without judgment, without criticism, without comment. Be with any feelings that come up as the child explains the fear and anger, and remember that this child is you, and that you once felt these feelings as strongly as this child does now.

(Pause)

Once the child has finished describing the fear or anger, thank your younger self for sharing with you. Tell your younger self about all of the fabulous things that s/he will do as s/he grows older, and describe how wonderful your adult life is. If you are feeling as if your adult life is NOT wonderful, don't talk about the negative things. Find one or two positive aspects of your life, and tell the child about the wonderful, competent, magical adult s/he grows up to be.

Tell the child that s/he doesn't have to feel afraid or angry anymore. Explain that now that you are a grown-up, you will handle the fearful situation and resolve it so that it no longer hurts the child. Reassure the child that it is safe to feel whatever s/he is feeling, and wish the child well. Remain in this energy for a few minutes.

(Pause)

As you remain alone in your safe place, ask yourself if the fear the child described is still with you. If so, thank the fear for its presence and its attempt to keep you safe. Explain to the fear that you no longer need it, and release it. It is important that you feel gratitude for the fear and that you understand that you have carried it with you all these years to protect you. Now that you are an adult, you no longer need the protection. Thank the fear, and let it go.

(Pause)

Once you've released the fear, say goodbye to your safe place. You may come back and visit as often as you like. Take one last look around, breathe deeply, and bring your awareness back to the room.

You may do this meditation as frequently as you need to, and you will probably need to do it fairly often. The fears that have been ingrained by well-meaning parents, grandparents, teachers, and guardians are hard to release once we become capable adults. The purpose of this meditation is to uncover childhood fears and let them go, once and for all. I encourage you to keep at it.

The Purpose of Your Emotions

We frequently mix up the terms "feelings" and "emotions." Feelings are the signals that we get from our bodies and our intuition. They are the sensations that give us feedback about our bodies and our minds. When you touch a hot stove, you get the *feeling* of a burn. When you have a thought that doesn't contribute to your well-being, you get a negative feeling. Emotions, on the other hand, are the meanings you ascribe to feelings. Emotions are "energy in motion." An uncomfortable sensation may lead to an emotional response that shuts you down and makes you less likely to interact with people. A pleasing feeling may cause an emotion of joy or friendliness. Although we use the words interchangeably, feelings are the actual sensation and emotions are the meaning we've given to those feelings.

In order to focus your emotions, you must learn to train your thoughts. Quantum physics and the Law of Attraction tell us that our life is a mirror image of the pictures we hold in our consciousness. That means that pushing against something you don't want won't make it go away. On the contrary, it will bring more of it into your experience. For example, if I say to you, "Don't think about pink elephants," what immediately comes to your mind? Another example is this—don't think about your left foot. What did you immediately think about? Your left foot was there all along, sending you signals that your mind filtered into the background. Once you focused your attention on it, those feelings came to the foreground. It is only by *ignoring* unwanted conditions that they disappear. Easier said than done, you say? Yes, it is. You have practiced your current thought pattern for an entire lifetime. It won't disappear overnight.

It will disappear very soon, however, if you replace it with a new thought pattern consistently. Scientists at NASA found that it takes only thirty days of consistently practicing a new habit before your brain adopts a new way of thinking.* In an experiment to see how astronauts would handle the lack of gravity in space, NASA engineers had astronauts wear goggles that made everything appear upside-down. The astronauts wore the goggles twenty-four hours a day, seven days a week, for one month. Although the experiment was meant to gauge the level of nausea and other physiological reactions to anti-

---

* Jack Canfield and Janet Switzer, *The Success Principles: How to Get from Where You Are to Where You Want to Be* (New York: Harper Collins, 2006).

gravity, the scientists found an unintended implication. After about twenty-five to thirty days, the astronauts' brains automatically inverted the image so that everything appeared to be right-side-up again. It took just under thirty days to retrain the brain to think in a different way. If you're feeling overwhelmed at the idea of trying to correct a lifetime of fear-based thinking, just recognize that you need to do it for only thirty days, and your brain will take over from there.

You might be asking, "How on earth am I going to monitor every thought I have?" Your brain has millions of thoughts every day, and only a tiny fraction of those are conscious. This is where your emotions enter the picture. Keeping track of every thought is practically impossible. Instead, you must tune into your emotions. Your emotions are a barometer of your thoughts. They tell you if the things you are thinking are positive or negative by the way they make you feel. If your self-talk is critical, angry, and fearful, you feel worse than if you were sending yourself loving, positive messages. It is crucial that you check in with your emotions on a regular basis. Once you've identified what you're feeling, you must try to reach for a better feeling-emotion. In their wonderful book *Ask and It Is Given*, Jerry and Esther Hicks call the emotional monitoring structure the Emotional Guidance System.* They provide a list of twenty-two emotions ranging from depression/despair to love/bliss/appreciation, and urge us to strive for the next best feeling-emotion on the scale.

To do this, we first identify our current emotion. Once we identify where we are, we can work our way up the scale, step

---

* For an excellent discussion of emotions, see Jerry and Esther Hicks in *Ask and It Is Given: Learning to Manifest Your Desires* (Carlsbad, CA: Hay House, 2004), 113–126.

by step. According to Jerry and Esther Hicks, we can't jump from depression to joy in one step, but we can move up the scale gradually. If you feel depression, then striving for anger will bring relief. Don't try to put a happy face on what you're feeling—it isn't real and it won't serve you in the long run. Just try to reach for the next best feeling-emotion, even if that emotion doesn't sound very good. Blame is better than anger, and contentment is better than blame. I spent months trying to reach up to boredom, because it was higher on the scale than pessimism, where I'd been for quite a while. I strongly urge you to get their book and become familiar with the Emotional Guidance System because it is one of your most useful keys to unlocking ongoing success.

Forgiveness

One of the most important ways to improve our emotional energy is forgiveness. Once you've identified where you are on the emotional scale, you can't move beyond fear and anger until you are willing to forgive. Forgiveness is a loaded topic for many people. As humans, we have developed an amazingly powerful desire to be right. When most people hear the word "forgiveness," they immediately assume that they are conceding their righteousness and admitting to being wrong. That position misses the fundamental purpose of forgiveness. We forgive to make ourselves feel better, not to let other people off the hook.

Spiritual teachers throughout the ages have recognized forgiveness as a powerful tool to get what we want. The premise behind the power of forgiveness is that staying angry doesn't hurt the other person—it hurts you. Based on what we have learned so far about the power of toxic emotions and the Law of Attraction, you know that being angry is not conducive to your long-term success. Staying angry at someone is like taking poison and expecting it to kill the other person. It just doesn't work that way.

Forgiving doesn't mean condoning the other person's behavior, or excusing their treatment of you. It also doesn't mean that you continue to put yourself in a situation where you can be hurt. You must set strong, healthy boundaries to keep yourself emotionally and physically safe, but once you've done that, release your anger and try to find a place of compassion for the person who hurt you.

One way to find compassion is to put yourself in the other person's shoes. We all make mistakes, and sometimes we hurt other people, usually unintentionally. That's probably true for the person who hurt you. We get so wrapped up in ourselves that we rarely stop to think about how our actions affect other people. If you are certain that someone hurt you deliberately, think again. They were probably just clueless. Even if they *did* hurt you deliberately, they were acting from their own pain and fear.

What about the really big things? What about the person who abused you as a child, who raped you, who cheated you, who beat you? Okay, what about them? Always remember that their actions were about *them*, not you. If you have had one of these experiences or a similar one, you are carrying a lot of anger. The anger has probably become a habituated pattern, so ingrained in your thought process that you don't even recognize it anymore. Let me ask you this: Is that anger, that fear, that loathing, hurting the other person? Is s/he suffering for your rage? Probably not, but you most certainly are.

Let's go back to the introduction, where we looked at the Simontons' findings in their work with cancer patients. The Simontons found that anger, fear, stress, and worry have two distinct effects on your body's chemistry. First, those emotions increase your body's production of abnormal and mutated cells. Second, the biochemicals of these emotions decrease your body's production of white blood cells, which are the basis of your immune system. When you feel anger, hurt, fear, and rage, you are increasing the number of abnormal cells in your body at the very same time you are decreasing your body's ability to dispose of those abnormal cells through the immune system. Let's look at an example unrelated to health. Holding on to anger clouds our judgment and impairs our decisions. I know people who *refused* to follow their dreams because it would have meant conceding that a former teacher or parent might have been right, even if they hadn't spoken to the person in decades. So let me ask again—who suffers when you hang on to old hurts? Go to therapy, confront the person, see a priest, take yoga classes, go on a meditation retreat—do whatever it takes, but forgive.

How to forgive varies by each individual, but in every case, it is releasing anger and resentment and recognizing the perfection in the situation. In his book *Radical Forgiveness*, author Colin Tipping suggests that every situation is divinely ordained and that we co-create the scenarios that hurt us in order for our souls to learn. According to Tipping, our souls made a contract to experience abuse, rejection, anger, or other negative emotions so that we could transform the energy through love. As the title of the book suggests, this is a radical viewpoint, but by accepting that we took part in the situation, even on an unconscious or preconscious level, we can release our perspective as a victim and come to a new understanding of the situation.*

What happens when the person you need to forgive most is yourself? This is probably the toughest act of forgiveness we have to perform, and the most crucial to healing. Find compassion for yourself, and keep yourself focused on the present and future, not the past. Remember that whatever transgression you committed, whatever action requires forgiveness, you did the best you could at the time.

We are evolving beings. Our consciousness is always changing and growing. You are not the same person today that you were five years ago, and you were not the same person then that you were five years before that. The decisions you made in the past are a reflection of who you were then, not who you are now. If you are wise, you will learn and grow from the mistakes you made, but you can't begin to learn or grow until you forgive yourself and find a way to objectively seek the lesson in each experience. Holding on to anger, berating yourself, denying yourself happiness and health, and otherwise punishing yourself are not ways to grow from the mistakes of your past. The only way to get beyond those events is forgiveness.

Forgiveness gets you focused on the present, not the past. Your power lies in the present moment, right here, right now. In order to focus on the present, you must heal the past. You can't change the past. You can't undo the things you have done, or the things that someone else did to you. You can only move

* Colin C. Tipping, *Radical Forgiveness: Making Room for the Miracle*, 2nd ed. (Wheaton, IL: Quest Books, 2002).

forward. Forgiveness is the only way to let go of the emotional ties that keep you rooted in old patterns of behavior.

Georgia* provides a spectacular illustration of the power of forgiveness. At age forty-two she was diagnosed with ovarian cancer. She underwent chemotherapy and was in remission for eight years, only to have a recurrence. She had more chemo, but the cancer came back a third time. The last recurrence forced Georgia to look closely at the emotions behind her cancer. She realized that she was carrying a lot of grief and anger. Georgia had been married but never had children because her husband didn't want them. She realized that she believed that her husband's refusal to have children was a reflection of his feelings toward her—that she wasn't good enough to bear his children. Although Georgia and her husband divorced, she was still angry at him. She realized her recurrences were part of her continued resentment. After her third round of chemo, she was ready to forgive. Now, she is in remission and optimistic for the future. She has amazed her doctors by the speed of her recovery. Forgiveness can work miracles.

Gratitude

In addition to forgiveness, spiritual teachers throughout the ages have shown that gratitude is the key to creating the life we want. Let's see how that works, specifically. Gratitude and appreciation release chemicals in the brain that cause a sense of well-being. These chemicals include serotonin and other endorphins that slow our heart rate, make our breathing more

---

* The person and story are real, but the name has been changed to protect privacy. Story used with permission.

efficient, and increase our body's production of white blood cells. Simply put, when you are in a state of gratitude, you are healthier than when you are in a state of fear.

Let's take that one step further. When you feel gratitude, it is impossible to feel fear or anger. Gratitude forces your attention onto the present moment and brings a feeling of peacefulness. How many times a day do you stop to appreciate the moment? Whatever you feel grateful for increases in proportion to your appreciation of it. Try it yourself. Find something, anything, that gives you a feeling of gratitude. Maybe it's your children or your home or a possession. Think about it and be grateful for it. Did you get some relief from the fear and worry while you were in that state of gratitude? If you didn't, ask yourself, "Was I really appreciating it?" Be honest.

Gratitude helps you gain power from your situation in several ways. First, we are never more grateful for what we have than when we are at risk of losing it. Whatever challenge you are facing is making very clear to you what you do want out of life. Second, experiencing gratitude teaches us to live in the moment and consciously choose our thoughts and feelings. Third, if you live in a constant state of gratitude, your attitudes will shift and you can heal the conditions in your life. Living in a constant state of anger or worry pinches off your well-being, but gratitude reverses that and promotes healing on all levels.

It all comes back to the Law of Attraction and your Emotional Guidance System. The world is a giant mirror, reflecting our attitudes in the circumstances that come into our lives. When you feel ill at ease, you are attracting more of that condition. When you feel joy, harmony, peace, and balance, you are attracting more of those, as well. By living in the moment and practicing gratitude, you increase the moments you feel well and decrease the moments you feel badly, therefore attracting more of your Good to you.

You might ask, how can I feel gratitude when things around me are so bad? This is at the heart of making peace with where you are. The simple answer is that you must look for the good things in your experience and ignore the bad. You must take your attention off anything that does not make you feel good. You must focus on those things in your life that create feelings of peace and harmony. Look for the good and praise it. This takes discipline in your thinking, but what is discipline, really, if not being a disciple? This may sound Pollyannaish, but what do you have to gain by focusing on the negatives? And what do you have to lose by not?

Try starting a gratitude journal. Every day, write down five to ten things that you appreciate about your life. This may seem difficult, especially if you're consumed with worry, fear, and anger. Perhaps you can start with being grateful that you recognized your challenging situation before it got any worse. You can feel grateful that you have the opportunity to change your life, or that you have new information from this book. Whatever works for you, try it. Do not stop until you have at least five things that you are grateful for, and it would be better if you had ten. I have found that some days, especially when things haven't gone well for me, I have to revert to my old standbys. These are things that I'm always grateful for, like my brilliant and talented daughter, my perfect health, my cozy home, my cute, dependable, and sporty car, the money I have in the bank, and my close-knit group of friends. No matter how bad a day I'm having, I can always stop and feel gratitude for these aspects of my life.

The key to gratitude journaling is that you must really get into the feeling of gratitude. Don't just pay lip service to your life's blessings. You'll get the most benefit if you allow the appreciation to well up inside you. This changes your internal chemistry and sends a signal to the universe that you are a person who appreciates getting gifts. It also shifts your focus and helps you remove your attention from the bad things that are happening. You can't get to where you want to be if you are stuck thinking over and over and over about where you don't want to be.

Acceptance

Acceptance is the logical outcome of facing fear, identifying your emotions, exercising forgiveness, and expressing gratitude. Eventually, you will get to the place where you are reconciled with where you are, right here, right now. You currently have a spectacular opportunity to reframe your experience, but you can't do that if you are in a state of condemning, regretting, or wishing. You are here, now. You are able to make choices going forward about what you want, and how you will shape your life to correspond with the success you desire. But you must start from where you are and have faith in your power to create a different reality.

Don't wait until something happens to practice these principles. Don't wait to forgive until you're through the divorce. Don't wait to start a gratitude journal until you have more money in the bank. Don't think that you have too much on your mind right now to try something new—that's exactly the point! The things you have on your mind are the fear-based thoughts that are contributing to your condition. Waiting for the right conditions before you start something is like waiting for the fireplace to get warm before you put wood in it. You want to replace those things with new thoughts and ideas that will empower your future. Accept where you are. Face your fears and let them go. Bless those who have hurt you and release them. Be grateful for the things you have, and know that with gratitude, you will get more. Above all, make peace with where you are.

Step 1 Worksheet

1. Get a journal and close your eyes. Feel the sensations you have in your body right now. How do you feel? Write down all the areas where you feel tension.

2. Ask your body what it's trying to tell you. Write down whatever comes into your mind.

3. What do you fear? Write down everything that causes you to feel the fear sensations in your body, including a racing heart, heavy breathing, sweating, dry mouth, and muscle tension. List current fears and old fears. Take plenty of time to do this—don't rush through it. If other fears surface in the next few days, go to your journal and write those down as well. You can't overcome what you're not aware of.

4. Get in touch with your Emotional Guidance System. I highly recommend getting *Ask and It Is Given* by Jerry and Esther Hicks, either from the library or a bookstore. The emotional scale is found on page 114. If you don't have the book, however, you can still tap into how you are feeling.

Close your eyes and be still. Ask yourself what emotion you have this very moment. Identify the emotion both by name and by the feeling in your body. Then, find a slightly better feeling-emotion. For example, if you're feeling depression or despair, try to feel angry instead. That seems counterintuitive, but you can't jump from despair to happiness all at once. All you can do is reach for the next best feeling-emotion. By reaching for anger, you are replacing the powerlessness of fear with the power of anger. Once you begin to feel power, you've moved yourself up the emotional scale.

5. Ask yourself, "Whom do I need to forgive today?" After you ask the question, close your eyes and wait for a picture to come to your mind. When you see the person's face, silently bless him/her and say that you understand that s/he was doing the best s/he could at the time, and that you release him/her from your hurt and anger. Find compassion for the person as you do this. This exercise may take some repeating. I suggest that you do it daily, so that you stay clear and don't allow negative emotions to reclog the pipeline.

6. Practice acceptance today. Whenever something occurs that upsets you, stop and breathe. Then repeat to yourself, "I accept this situation and let go of my need to control it." In the next section we will discuss how you can respond to events in order to bring about the outcomes you desire, but for now, just breathe and accept whatever is happening. Getting angry or fearful in the moment won't change the situation; it will only keep you mired in negativity. As you go through the day, become a detached observer of events, and release your need for control.

7. Start a gratitude journal. Every day, write between five and ten things that you appreciate in your life. You can write more than ten if you like—the more you write, the better you'll feel. We attract whatever we put our attention toward. If we focus on the things that make us feel good, we will attract more of that. Instead of focusing on adversity, be grateful for the Good that you *do* have, and you will attract more of it.

Meditation—Tuning into Your Body

Get into a relaxed position and concentrate on your breath. Release any tension you feel. Focus on the working of your body. Become conscious of your lungs filling with air as you inhale, then squeezing out the breath on the exhale. Imagine your lungs as clean, shiny bellows that work with impeccable precision to bring in the perfect amount of air, filter it, and deliver the oxygen to the bloodstream. Visualize them working perfectly to bring life force to every cell of your body.

(Pause)

Become conscious of your bloodstream. "Feel" the blood flowing through every part of your body, and imagine it flowing through and nourishing all your internal organs. Picture your white and red blood cells moving with the bloodstream. Imagine them patrolling for foreign substances and toxins, and then dissolving those foreign substances on contact. They act as the police, keeping the riffraff out of your bloodstream.

(Pause)

Now picture your heart beating rhythmically. Feel it pumping energy into your limbs, your organs, your brain. Match your breathing to the pumping of the heart, and feel gratitude that it works tirelessly and impeccably to circulate blood throughout your body.

(Pause)

Become aware of any tension that you are holding in your body. If the muscles in your neck, back, legs, or arms feel tight, relax and release them. Let any stiffness melt away into the ground. Feel the sensation of letting go. It may feel like you are floating, or becoming weightless. Stay in this weightless feeling as long as you can, focusing on your breathing, allowing any thoughts that enter your mind to pass right through.

(Pause)

Now, repeat silently to yourself, "Peace." Anytime an unwanted thought enters your mind, breathe into it, allow it to float through and out of your consciousness, and silently say, "Peace." Stay in this state for about five minutes, until you are totally relaxed.

(Pause)

When you feel complete with the process, take a final deep breath, say "Peace" one last time, and bring your awareness back to the room.

STEP 2

Take Responsibility

Wherever you go, there you are.
—ANONYMOUS

Now that you've made peace with where you are, it's time to figure out the role you played in your current adversity. At first, we don't want to hear that we've played any role in what's happening. Whether we have a business that's in trouble, a marriage that's failing, or a serious health crisis, we like to think that we are the victims here. However, you can't hope to have things get better until you realize that you helped create the situation. You can't change what you can't control. By acknowledging that you played a role in the onset of the situation, you have the ability to facilitate a resolution.

Responsibility versus Victimhood

I want to be very clear here that taking responsibility is not the same as laying blame. Blame connotes anger, fear, and wrongdoing. Taking responsibility is not about pronouncing a situation right or wrong. Rather, you must understand that you made choices and took action that created the situation you have now. Frequently, when I talk to clients about taking responsibility for their challenges, they immediately get defensive: "I didn't wish this upon myself." They get angry at me for insinuating that they played any role at all in their situation and usually fall into the victim mode.

It is really easy to be a victim. Victims don't have to take responsibility for anything. Victims can point to the outside world and say that "they" have created the situation. Victims don't have to leave their comfort zones or risk being embarrassed, hurt, or rejected. Victims also don't have any control over their lives. They live in constant fear and anger because they feel helpless to correct the negative situations around them.

As humans, we are reluctant to see our own dysfunctional patterns. If you've spent thirty, forty, or fifty years creating an identity, you're very much in a comfort zone. When something happens to threaten that identity, whether it is retirement, loss of a job, a divorce, kids leaving home, or some other major event, the comfort zone shatters and you have to step in and take responsibility for the next phase of your life. Many people have trouble with this, however. They get into a rut, and believe that their circumstances are dictated by external factors. They may be angry about those circumstances, or fearful of them, but they don't see a way to change them. This creates victim thinking. Victims are unwilling to take action to change their situation. Sometimes, they don't know what action needs to be taken, and sometimes they do know but are afraid to take the risk. They feel trapped by circumstances.

The pattern of victimhood is prevalent in today's society. We de-emphasize personal responsibility in our home lives, schools, and workplaces. Our legal system is bogged down with lawsuits filed by people who engaged in self-destructive behavior, like smoking cigarettes for decades, and now want the tobacco industry to take responsibility for their poor health. Our school system blames teachers because students can't read, without looking at the responsibility of the student or his/her parents. We always have choices, however, and we create everything in our lives.

In his book *The Success Principles*, Jack Canfield provides a great example of taking responsibility for unwanted situations. You go into a bar and find the biggest, toughest-looking guy there. You see that he has obviously been drinking for a long time and is acting unpredictably. Still, you walk up to him and say, "You're ugly!"—and you end up in the hospital with a broken jaw. You may want to sue the big guy at the bar, but you created that situation.*

Here's a less obvious example. You live an unhappy life for years. You continue to work at a job you hate because you don't see how else you can support your family. You stay in an unhappy marriage because you're afraid of being alone. You eat unhealthy foods and watch television instead of exercising because you feel sorry for yourself that you have such a miserable life. Then you're diagnosed with cancer, and you feel helpless and victimized because this aggressor has invaded your body. You created that situation, too.

You can't continue to think like a victim and expect to be powerful. You can't change what you can't control. Once

---

* Jack Canfield and Janet Switzer, *The Success Principles: How to Get from Where You Are to Where You Want to Be* (New York: Harper Collins, 2006).

you realize the part you played in your current experience of adversity, you have great power to overcome it. What we create, we can change. Until we accept this basic truth, we remain powerless.

E + R = O

There's an extremely useful formula that I've encountered over the years in a variety of places: E + R = O. Event plus Response equals Outcome. This formula illustrates how each of us is responsible for the conditions in our lives. Life throws situations at us all the time. Quantum physicists would argue that we attract these situations to us, but regardless of how situations get to us, stuff happens. Some of it is beyond our awareness, some of it we may have seen coming, but it still throws us a curve ball when it arrives. Your life is a series of Events, which elicit from you a series of Responses, which in turn create your Outcomes. You are never a victim. Life may have given you uncomfortable events, and you may have made some poor choices, but you were never completely passive in anything that happened.

This simple formula is also reflected in the Eastern teaching of karma. Karma is really just the law of cause and effect. It says that you cause things to happen based on your choices. Karma deals with the Response and the Outcome, claiming that you bring things into being based on your beliefs and choices. Karma is frequently misconstrued to mean some sort of pre-determination or cosmic punishment for things you did in a past life, but truly the concept isn't that mystical. Karma just states that you make choices (cause), and those choices have consequences (effect). To use our terminology, you have a Response (cause) to an Event, and that creates the Outcome (effect).

Most people don't like to hear that they've made poor choices. Accepting responsibility brings up all sorts of negative emotions like embarrassment, blame, shame, and self-loathing. These are uncomfortable emotions, and no one likes to feel them. But they are still part of your emotional package, and you have them as an indicator that you are thinking and doing things that hurt your overall well-being. Facing these emotions is crucial to being able to take responsibility for your current situation.

This is where the forgiveness we talked about in Step 1 comes in. If you have forgiven yourself for all of the things you think you've done wrong, it's easier to step up to the plate and take responsibility without being debilitated by shame and fear. Remember, nothing you have ever done in your life is so bad that you can't forgive yourself for it. You have always done the best you could at the time. You may feel that you didn't do the best you were capable of, but that is different from doing the best that you could. If you didn't live up to your potential at times, it was because you had something else holding you back, whether it was fear, guilt, anger, shame, rage, or helplessness. When you factor together all of your feelings and all of your responses, you did the best you could at the time.

People also are afraid of the word "responsibility" because it brings up feelings of unworthiness or inadequacy. Think of the word as a compound of the words "response" and "ability." You have the ability to control your response to every situation.

You have the power to respond in whatever way necessary to bring about the outcome you desire. By taking responsibility, you are claiming that you are able to respond. All it takes is a shift of focus from "I can't because" thinking, which is victim-thinking, to "Here's what I'll do."

Let's talk briefly again about the Law of Attraction, which brings events that match the thoughts and feelings you have and the images you hold in your mind. Your thoughts have a certain frequency, and you attract situations, people, and things that correspond to that frequency. If you have spent a lifetime thinking like a victim, you will be a victim. The anti-dote is very simple—just change the way you think. It may sound simple, but it's not easy. However, it is possible.

Let's look a little deeper at the E + R = O formula. Quantum physics claims that there can be no universe without someone to observe it. In other words, an object does not exist without an observer. No doubt you have heard the conundrum, "If a tree falls in the forest and there is no one there to hear it, does it make a sound?" Quantum physicists would say not only that it does not, but they would also say that the tree would not even exist unless there was someone there to see it. Stick with me here. All of life is energy, and energy can shift in and out of form based upon the expectations of the observer. Einstein's theory of relativity, $E=MC2$, proves this idea. The equation basically shows that energy equals matter multiplied by a constant, in this case, the speed of light squared. Therefore, matter is just energy in a different form.

This is an abstract and difficult concept to understand, but once you grasp it, it gives you amazing control, and amazing responsibility, over your life. Basically, you create the situations and conditions of your life by the way you observe them. All possible outcomes to any situation exist simultaneously in the quantum field. That means that the possibility of your perfect life is already out there. Unfortunately, the possibility of your public disgrace or untimely death is out there, as well. Do you remember the television series *Star Trek*? Sometimes the crew visited alternate realities where they experienced what their life would have been like if they'd made different choices. Think of your life as alternate realities existing at the same time.

So how do you know which reality will actually happen? Will you live a long and happy life, or will your current situation completely destroy you? Here's the radical part—it is your choice. You might ask, "How can it be my choice? Why on earth would I choose option #2?" The answer is that you wouldn't—consciously. But many people are unconscious or misinformed about the way the world works. You attract experiences based on the thoughts you think and the images you hold in your mind, whether they are conscious or unconscious. If you spend all your mental energy worrying about being sick, broke, or alone, you will attract more of sick, broke, or alone. This is the Law of Attraction at work.

The Law of Attraction doesn't make judgments like "good" or "bad," "right" or "wrong." It just brings you what you think about the most. If you are spending all of your time worrying and envisioning miserable outcomes, you are attracting those very things into your experience. You must remove your attention from the condition you don't want. That means you must not think about it at all. Easier said than done, you say? Yes, it takes practice, but you can learn techniques to keep your mind focused on the outcome you *want* to experience, rather than the one you don't.

Visualize Supportive Choices

The most powerful technique to attract what you want is visualization. In their years of clinical research with cancer patients, the Simontons found that more than two-thirds of their terminal patients who used visualization beat the prognosis and survived. When I was sick, I visualized three times a day. I would go to a quiet place and see my white blood cells eating up any cancer cells they encountered. I also visualized my life after cancer. I saw myself as strong, healthy, at my ideal weight, able to do all the activities I wanted. Within three years of going into remission, I was at a weight and size that I had never been in my life, and was running 10K road races and climbing mountains. I never could have done those things with my body if I hadn't first gone there in my mind.

Entrepreneur and teacher John Assaraf tells a wonderful story that illustrates the power of visualization. He created a vision board with a picture of his dream house on it and looked at it every day for a year, until he packed it away for a cross-country move. During the next few years, he moved several places, ultimately buying a home. As the family was settling in, his young son was helping him unpack the boxes in his office and asked about his old vision boards. As Assaraf explained them to his son, he looked at the vision board he hadn't seen in five years and realized for the first time that he was actually *living* in the dream home he had pictured on the board.

Similarly, actor Jim Carrey used the technique of visualization after having struggled financially during his early life, at one time even living with his family in a camper. Then when he began acting, he wrote a check to himself for $10 million and dated it Thanksgiving, 1995. He carried it around in his wallet as he continued to get acting jobs, each one paying a little more and a little more until right before Thanksgiving, 1995, when he was hired to play the role in *Dumb and Dumber* for $10 million. That is the power of visualization.

One way to focus your thoughts is to write down what you want out of life. Don't limit it to just one specific goal. Write down the perfect life. Dream big! Ask for what you've always wanted. I wanted to be a writer as a child, but my parents drilled into my head that I couldn't make a living that way, so I gave up that dream. When I was sick, I realized that my dream included being a writer. I stopped making excuses and started writing a little bit, every day, and voilà! I've now published four books.

What dreams have you given up? What goals did you feel were too big? Write them down! Then, take five minutes, three times a day, and review your goals. Visualize yourself living the goals right here, right now. Get into the feeling of them, and do everything you can to experience the goals as if they were happening in the present. When you're not visualizing, daydream about having accomplished the goals. Get so excited about your goals that you can't wait to get started on them. This will distract your attention from worry and facilitate your success.

Visualizing a supportive outcome helps us to make better choices. Instead of condemning our circumstances and wistfully thinking about how much better our lives would be if these things hadn't happened, we recognize we always have a choice. We can continue to blame the past—or we can stay focused on the outcome we *want*, by visualizing the life we want to create. Focusing on our desires helps us make healthier responses, thus creating healthier outcomes.

One man who took seriously the idea of taking responsibility had an amazing turnaround in his financial fortunes. Duane* owned a small business that had been doing all right for more than ten years but had never really thrived. When he remarried and started graduate school, he realized that he needed more income than his business could provide. At the same time, the economy was undergoing a downturn, and he noticed that business was drying up. The Event was that his business could no longer support him. His initial Response to this situation was to be in denial. He worked hard for the clients he had and kept trying to get more business, but there was still no improvement. He was the classic example of someone repeating the same behavior over and over while expecting different results.

At some point, he realized he had to do something differently, so his next Response was to focus on soliciting new clients. He was still very attached to the idea that he was being victimized by the economy and his own bad luck. He beat the bushes, asked current clients if they needed any additional services, and stayed hopeful that things would turn around. They did not. His income continued to decline, putting tremendous pressure on the household finances and his new marriage. Not

---

* The person and story are real, but the name has been changed to protect privacy. Story used with permission.

only did it look as if he was going to have to drop out of graduate school, but he was having trouble making his car payment. He got so behind in his bills that he started locking his car in the garage so it wouldn't get repossessed.

Throughout this time, friends suggested that perhaps Duane should get a job. He was reluctant, however, because he felt he just wasn't the corporate type. He'd had corporate jobs in the past and didn't feel as if he fit in that structure. Also, Duane had been self-employed for almost fourteen years and really loved the freedom of making his own hours and having a flexible schedule. He felt victimized by his situation and believed that if he could just hang on through the economic downturn, he'd be okay. He reinvigorated his efforts to get more clients.

After a few more months of that, however, Duane's financial situation was finally at the breaking point. He was behind in car payments, child support, and every other bill. No matter how hard he worked to get new clients, there was simply no work to be had. He finally began to envision a life in which he was able to pay his bills, which helped him choose a different Response.

Reluctantly, Duane began to apply for jobs. He was uncertain what to even apply for, since it had been a long time since he'd worked for someone else, and his business was somewhat eclectic. He started sending out résumés, however, realizing that he had to take responsibility for his own financial success and the well-being of his family. As he was in the process of job hunting, a friend mentioned that she was leaving her temporary job and the company was looking to replace her. Although it wasn't the field in which Duane was looking, it was a job he had done before and therefore had experience. He ended up interviewing for it and got the job on a temporary basis, which turned into a permanent position a few months later. More importantly, by taking responsibility for his own situation, he was able to find a new career path that turned out to be rewarding, both financially and spiritually.

Are you afraid to say no? Do you worry more about pleasing other people than pleasing yourself? These are some of the choices you must recognize as part of taking responsibility. Most Americans find it difficult to put themselves first. As the universal caregivers, women are expected to sacrifice their time, careers, bodies, and health to take care of children, parents, spouses, and society at large. Men, on the other hand, are expected to bottle up feelings, fix everything, and earn money to support the family. Both genders have trouble saying no to activities that don't serve their well-being when they fall within these prescribed gender roles.

Also, we humans are pretty nice people. We don't want to hurt anyone's feelings, cause disappointment, or fail to meet expectations. To that end, we say yes to all sorts of things that we'd rather not do, all to avoid the unpleasantness of hurting someone else. Have you ever avoided ending a bad relationship because you didn't want to be the bad guy? Or gone to an event or activity that you really dreaded because you didn't want to disappoint the person who invited you? Or played games with your children after an exhausting day at work, when what you really wanted to do was curl up and read a book? Heck, I kept going to bad hair stylists for years because I didn't want to hurt their feelings! These are choices that we make in each moment that do not lead us to success.

We also tend to be a codependent culture. We look outside ourselves for happiness and expect other people to read our minds. We expect our spouse to know when we need to be held, our children to know when we need some quiet time, our employer to know when we need some time off, and our friends to know when we want to do something. We have a terrible aversion to asking for what we want and taking care of our own needs. The emotional crisis brought on by your current adversity is a signal that this pattern must stop.

You are a big girl or boy now. You have the power to make your own choices about how to care for yourself. You must first decide that you are worthy of your own well-being. You are worthy of time off. You are worthy of self-nurturing. You are worthy of being healthy and worthy of taking care of yourself. You are worthy of being loved and prosperous. You don't have to run yourself ragged to prove your own worth. You must accept that you are worthy just by being on the planet.

Once you acknowledge your worthiness, you must make choices accordingly. Let go of your responsibility to everyone else, and increase your responsibility to yourself. People treat us the way we teach them to treat us. We frequently don't have enough respect for ourselves to demand proper treatment. This is a condition that probably began in childhood. If you watch the way many parents raise their children, they demand respect from the child, but don't give the child respect in return. For example, children are told to not interrupt their parents, but parents interrupt their children all the time. Thus we learn early on that we don't deserve respect. If you want to succeed, that must change.

There are some exercises in the worksheet at the end of this step that will help you with respect, but know for now that you must respect your own desires enough to make choices that serve you. This means choosing to take a morning off work if you're tired and need to rest. It means getting a babysitter if you've had a hard day or week at work and need some time alone. It means asking your spouse to create an equitable division of labor around the house if you feel that the burden is falling mostly on you. It means hiring a financial planner to help with money priorities. Most of all, making supportive choices means honoring the messages your body and emotions are giving you, and acting accordingly. Have you ever noticed that you get more emotional when you're tired? Or that you're cranky when you feel that you've worked harder than everyone else? Or that you become depressed when you feel trapped by a situation with no immediate way out? These are the subtle emotional and physical dynamics that tell us that we're out of alignment with our Good. By tuning into the way you feel, and making choices that will make you feel better in the moment, you are practicing self-respect and acting in a healthy way.

Making supportive emotional choices also means exercising your personal power. We are more powerful than we can imagine, but we are frequently afraid to use our power. We look for people and circumstances outside of ourselves to make choices for us, rather than deciding what we want and standing up for it. If you're facing a health challenge like cancer, remember that your oncologist is the expert on the scientific aspects, but YOU are the expert on your body. If you are in a difficult relationship, you need to clearly decide what you want and ask for it, rather than waiting for your partner to read your mind. If you're facing a financial difficulty, remember there is always enough money to have what you want, as long as you want what you have. Do you shop to make yourself feel better?

Are you happy with your possessions? Can you give anything up? Make the supportive choice to get clear on what you want and stand firm in that knowledge.

The great mystics have all talked about the power of choice. Most of the parables in the Bible are about choices and their potential outcomes. Most New Thought teachers talk about the power of intention, which is really just making a choice. We always have the power to choose the out-come we want to experience. Even when we don't choose, we've still made a choice—we've chosen to let circumstances dictate our out-come, rather than take responsibility ourselves. There is no such thing as a victim. We always have a choice, and whether we exercise that choice or not is, well, our choice.

I had to take responsibility for my own health care and make some difficult choices, even in the face of opposition from my doctors. When I was going through chemotherapy, the chemicals ate through my white blood cells very quickly. Consequently, I had to give myself injections of a drug called Neupogen to stimulate my body's production of white blood cells. My regimen called for me to have a chemo treatment every fourteen days. My oncologist prescribed that I inject myself with Neupogen days 4 through 9 of the cycle, so that my white blood cells would be elevated enough on day 14 for me to have the next infusion. The first time we tried this, however, my white blood cell count peaked on day 11 and then crashed again by day 14 and we had to postpone my treatment for a week. I was devastated and asked my doctor why he had me taking the Neupogen so early in my cycle. Why didn't I take it days 9 through 14? He informed me that I couldn't take Neupogen within three days of chemo—meaning I couldn't have an injection after day 11. I then asked him why we didn't vary the schedule so I took it days 6 through 11, and he told me to trust him, be patient, and it would work out.

For the next round, I did as he said, and again on day 14 my white blood count was too low, and we had to postpone chemo again. I was devastated again, but more importantly, I was angry. I had moved up the emotional scale from helplessness to anger—which gave me power. I just *knew* that I needed to take the Neupogen days 6 through 11. I could tell by the way my body felt that my white blood cells didn't crash until after day 7. I could tell by the pain in my bones that the Neupogen didn't last as long as the doctor thought it would. I knew from having lived in my body for thirty-three years that I process medication very quickly, and it takes more than normal to be effective on me. I decided to listen to my body and my intuition, working within the parameters the doctor set.

During the next cycle, I gave myself the Neupogen shots on days 6 through 11 rather than days 4 through 9. I asked the oncology nurse about it, but didn't tell my doctor. When I went in for chemo on day 14, my white blood cell count was perfect. "Well," my doctor said, "I told you it would work." I confessed that I'd done it my way, and the doctor just shrugged his shoulders and said, "Medicine isn't an exact science. You know your body best. Good for you." I took the shots days 6 through 11 for the rest of my treatment, and never had another problem. I'm not suggesting that anyone ignore a doctor's advice, but I am saying that we must always consult and honor our innate wisdom.

Don't give your emotional or physical power away to anyone. Remember that you are response-able. Listen to the experts, but listen to yourself, too. Get very clear on the outcome you want, and don't waver from it for a minute. Insist on being treated with love, kindness, respect, honor, and openness. In return, treat everyone you meet, most especially yourself, with the same qualities. Make your emotional choices based on this self-respect, love, and honor, and your intuition will help you use the cosmic 2x4 to hit a home run.

Step 2 Worksheet

1. In your journal, list five ways that you have acted like a victim in the past year.
2. Looking at the above list, write out alternate ways you could have responded that would have changed the outcome.
3. Make a list of all the things in your life that displease you. Whatever you're currently facing will understandably be at the top of this list. Next to each item, write the way you have responded to them and the outcome. Now write at least two alternate responses you could have had, and the possible outcome from each of those responses.
4. Write out your perfect life. Take some time to contemplate the things you want—relationships, health, career, possessions. These may be material things like a car or a house, or they can be intangible things like a perfect relationship, more peacefulness, or more quality time with your family. Write out your dream life in detail, and write it in present tense, as if it is happening now.
5. Based on your dream life, make a vision board or journal. Go through magazines, picture books, or the Internet, and find pictures of the things that you want. If your desire is

something intangible, find an image that evokes the feeling you will have when you've gotten it. Place the images on a bulletin board, your refrigerator door, or in a journal, and look at them every day. As you look at the images, imagine yourself having the goal right now. Picture how you will look, feel, and act when you have the things you desire. What would you do today if you were perfectly healthy? Had all the money you wanted? Worked at your dream job? How would you hold your head? How would you approach the day? Take five to ten minutes each day to do the visioning exercise.

6. Each night for the next thirty days, stand in front of a mirror and tell yourself, out loud, what you appreciate about yourself. Look into your eyes, and recite the good things you did that day. Be sure to mention the positive choices you made and acknowledge yourself for making them and staying in tune with your desires. This will feel awkward at first, but you'll get used to it. The important thing here is that you mention good things only. Don't spend any time at all on anything that didn't make you feel proud, capable, and focused. End by saying, "I love you."

7. In your journal, write out a typical day of your ideal life. What time would you get up? Where would you go each day? What would you spend your time doing? Who would you be with? What would your evenings be like? Once you've written your perfect day, write a list of five small things you can do to move closer to that vision. Start tomorrow to make different choices and do the five small things.

Meditation—Seeing the Future

Breathe deeply as you still your mind. Relax into your chair. Focus as you inhale and exhale. Imagine your heart, shiny and sparkly, radiating light out from you in all directions. Feel yourself surrounded by a circle of light. Know that the light brings strength, power, clarity, and focus.

(Pause)

Imagine the circle of light as a gigantic bubble, protecting you and surrounding you with well-being and strength. Feel the calm, peace, and joy brought on by being enveloped by light. Feel power rush through you.

(Pause)

Think of a time in the last year when you have not taken full responsibility for your actions. This may be in the area of your health, your relationships, your work, or another arena. Ask your inner being why you didn't take full responsibility. Was it fear? Insecurity? Anger? Do not judge the answer! Do not get upset with yourself for the reason—just observe and understand it. If you need to forgive yourself, do so now.

(Pause)

Next, imagine the bubble lifting you up from the earth and allowing you to float forward in time. From the bubble of light, you can go to any possible future outcome you want. Float forward a month, and take a moment to appreciate what you see. Imagine that you are looking down on the scene from above. What is the status of your health? How are your relationships? What are you doing with your days? Are you happy? Take a few moments to really see the picture below you.

(Pause)

Now float forward a year, then five years. At each milestone, take time to appreciate the scene below you. Really take it all in, and notice as many details as you can. Get the picture of your fabulous future firmly in your mind. Once you've done that, allow the bubble to float back to the present. Rest for a moment inside the safety of the bubble, and affix the picture you have of your future firmly in your consciousness.

(Pause)

When you can clearly see your future in a month, a year, and five years, ask yourself what choices you have to make right now to get to those ends. You don't have to change things overnight, but ask your inner being what five small steps you need to take today to move closer to your desired outcome. Remember that you are still surrounded by the protecting bubble of light, which represents the field of all possibilities. You can create any future you desire by your willingness to make choices.

(Pause)

Make a commitment to yourself to start today to do five small things toward your goal. Feel yourself being powerful and having the strength to accomplish whatever you decide to do. Feel the power and resolve surging through every cell of your body. Take a few moments to bask in your power. Remember, the bubble of light, the field of all possibilities, is always with you. When you are ready, return your awareness to the room.

STEP 3

Identify the Benefits

We create our reality as we go along.
—WINSTON CHURCHILL

Y ou're probably looking at the title of this chapter and won-
dering, "What could possibly be the benefit of what I'm
going through?" Believe it or not, your higher Transpersonal Self doesn't do *anything* unless there is some benefit to
you. As hard as that may be to accept in your current situation,
the universe is always trying to help you. Self-made millionaire and motivational guru W. Clement Stone called himself a
reverse paranoid—he believed the universe was conspiring to
help him, and he was right. We live in a benevolent universe.
You are facing your current challenge because there is some
benefit for you. Once you determine what that benefit is, you
will heal the situation.

The Path of Least Resistance

Everything in the universe works on the principle of least resistance. Look at nature. Everything happens with ease. Grass

doesn't strain to grow or water to flow. We are meant to have a great life, and it is meant to happen effortlessly. If it is not happening easily, it's because you are resisting the Good that is flowing to you. Old ideas of unworthiness, discouragement, or hopelessness have kept you from identifying and following the path of least resistance to your dreams. The current adversity you are facing is a way to show you how your thoughts and emotions have created turmoil and point you to the path of least resistance.

What causes emotional turmoil in your life? For most people, resistance comes from the negative emotions we've already talked about—fear, anger, shame, anxiety, hopelessness, and helplessness. As children, we had no resistance. Have you ever watched little kids play? They are carefree and focused on what they want. They have no inhibitions and very little fear. That's what makes the job of parenting such a challenge!

As we grow up, we learn to hide our feelings, along with our talents. We develop personas that don't always fit us. As we forego our talents and preferences and do things that are more acceptable to our social group, we create emotional resistance. Sometimes the resistance isn't severe, so we can live with it for thirty, forty, or fifty years before it starts to wear us out. Other times, the resistance is so severe that we can withstand the stress for only five, ten, or twenty years. It depends on each case, but in all cases, the resistance causes emotional pain. The way we handle this emotional pain can lead to non-supportive or self-destructive tendencies, which have undoubtedly contributed to the adversity in our lives.

In the case of physical challenges, the Simontons found that all their patients had some sort of dysfunctional upbringing. As children, these individuals learned to stop being who they naturally were and developed more acceptable personas in order to survive. In their youth, this meant denying or hiding their feelings to please grown-ups. Perhaps they had to stop being a kid and take care of their parents or siblings. In their young childhood, these personas were the path of least resistance, because they helped them survive in their situation. Many of us can relate to this pattern.

As the patients grew older, they carried these personas into their adult lives. Sometimes this meant that the budding artist put away her dreams and became a teacher or a nurse, or the burgeoning architect went into computer engineering instead. Perhaps they married someone they didn't love in order to please their parents, had children to keep peace with their spouse, or stayed in an unhappy relationship to avoid the insecurity of divorce. In each of these cases, the emotional choices they made were easier than facing their overarching fears, and so provided the path of least resistance at that moment.

These patterns are probably familiar to many of us. Hiding our true selves to please others becomes such second nature by the time we're adults that we hardly recognize we're doing it. At some point, however, the effort we've exerted to suppress our true selves takes a physical toll, and the knowledge of what we've given up takes an emotional toll. It's like writing with the non-dominant hand. If someone ties up your dominant hand and makes you write a report, writing with your non-dominant hand provides the path of least resistance for a time. If you keep writing with your non-dominant hand, however, it begins to wear you out. You aren't meant to write that way, and the fatigue and stress caused by having to concentrate so hard is your body's way of telling you something is wrong.

Extrapolate that metaphor and you can understand how adversity comes into our lives. The universal force of Good is always beckoning us to express our true selves. Before your current challenge, you probably had many clues that you were resisting. I'm sure there were times you felt that you needed to force a situation, or suck it up and put your desires on hold. Had you tuned into your emotions, you would have realized that you were probably feeling frustration, anger, maybe despair. You might have gotten small ailments that you ignored as your body tried to nudge you back into alignment, but you didn't listen. You probably had little setbacks that provided you with gentle ways of changing course. You kept doing what you'd always done because you couldn't quite figure out what else to do. Then you were delivered a cosmic 2x4.

I was in that situation. For years before my cancer diagnoses I was unhappy, but I couldn't put my finger on what was wrong, so I just kept doing what I'd always done. I was married to a handsome, successful, wonderful man, but we had no emotional connection. Still, I wouldn't leave the marriage because it wasn't *bad*. It just wasn't *good*, either. I gave up a career to go to graduate school so I could be home with any children we might have. I loved the subject I studied in graduate school, but the idea of becoming a full-time college professor didn't feel right. Still, there was nothing *wrong* with it, so I continued on the path. I was conflicted about being a mother because my upbringing taught me that being a mother meant sacrificing my true self. I loved my daughter, but I was resentful about giving up my hobbies, friends, free time, and relationships to be at her beck and call. I was unhappy to my core, but completely unprepared to correct the situation. The unhappiness was my clue that I was *resisting*.

My body tried to bring me back into alignment numerous times. I was always exhausted, and kept feeling as if I needed to rest. I thought that if I could just sleep for a few weeks, I could think more clearly. The energy it took to keep up the façade of being happy was becoming more than I could bear, but I was still unwilling to admit that perhaps my life wasn't working. I was so invested in *succeeding*—by struggling, trying, striving, suppressing, and resisting—that I forgot how to be happy.

My unhappiness showed in my body. In the twenty-four months before I was diagnosed with cancer, I had a series of mysterious ailments. I got dizzy spells that the doctor could never quite diagnose but claimed it was probably a viral inner ear infection. I suddenly developed eczema on my hands. I got strange rashes on my face and arms for no reason, and they would disappear as quickly as they came. I developed an allergy to walnuts, which I had never had before, and haven't had since finishing chemo. I got bronchitis twice and walking pneumonia once. Each time I refused to stop and evaluate my life. Instead, I kept up the resistance and continued to live in my persona. I was the perfect wife, perfect mother, and straight-A student, but I never asked if I was doing what I wanted. I refused to let these ailments slow me down. I continued to shove the round peg of my outward life into the square hole of my true desires. I was exhausted.

Finally, I developed the lump in my neck. Looking back, I'm grateful for it. I may have never re-evaluated my life if cancer hadn't caused me to look at how I was resisting. It took me years to see all the resistance, and I'm still finding meaning in it. I realized that I had refused to let myself do my true life's work. I refused to let myself be in a happy relationship because I was afraid of hurting my husband. It wasn't until I realized the disservice I was doing him that I finally told him how I really felt, only to find out that he felt the same way. We are now very happily divorced and have a positive relationship. Cancer allowed me to stop resisting my well-being—it stopped being the path of least resistance and showed me a better way.

I have noticed this same pattern in my personal financial challenges, relationship issues, and questions about my purpose. The universe provides subtle clues at first, but if I keep resisting, the messages get stronger and stronger until wham! Failed business! Divorce! Failing health! If only we could listen sooner, right?

Find the Hidden Emotions

Adversity becomes the path of least resistance because we are usually unaware that we are resisting. Many of us are taught as small children that we are not supposed to feel good: "No pain, no gain." If we are too joyful or carefree, we're accused of being lazy. This isn't really our parents' fault—they were raised the same way and truly believed they were helping us by teaching us that life must be hard. They were saving us from disappointment.

We probably were also taught to hide our emotions and act according to specific rules of society, regardless of how we really felt. There was a certain age where we became too old to cry. Boys, in particular, were discouraged from showing tenderness or true emotion because it is viewed as a sign of weakness. Conversely, women have been trained to swallow their anger and just "take it." Because of our great need for acceptance as children, we developed a protective emotional armor to hide these emotions. This is part of the development of our persona.

As we learned to act certain ways in order to get love, affection, approval, and protection from our parents, developing a persona usually meant hiding our true feelings.

As we got older, however, those feelings didn't want to stay hidden. Without a healthy outlet, those so-called negative emotions frequently expressed themselves in inappropriate ways. Taken to the extreme, anger can become homicide, depression, or suicide. In less dramatic examples, the successful young business-woman who was always the "good girl" starts to go out on the weekends and drink too much, which begins to affect her performance at work. The macho man who was told he couldn't cry builds up so much emotional pain that he begins drinking excessively to dull the feelings. Other disturbing behaviors that surface are addictions, promiscuity, verbal abuse of our children or spouse, and violence.

Most of us who experience these behaviors have no idea where they came from. We are at a loss as to why sometimes we seem so normal and other times we are so deviant. Our suppressed emotions have to find an outlet. They must manifest somewhere. Like a pressure cooker, if we keep the lid on our feelings indefinitely, the pressure will build up and the feelings will eventually blow.

Physical ailments are ways that the pressure is released. Our physical bodies provide an outlet for our emotions, and we develop illnesses to give the energy of our suppressed emo-tions a place to let loose. In order to maintain perfect wellness, we cannot continue to ignore and deny how we feel. We have to uncover the hidden emotions that make us sick and find healthy and productive outlets for them.

In her path-breaking book *You Can Heal Your Life*, author Louise L. Hay explains how limiting beliefs are often the cause of physical illness.* Hay goes into great detail about the ways that different beliefs manifest in the body and create illness. Accord-ing to Hay, the thoughts we have about ourselves manifest through our subconscious minds to create physical symptoms in our bodies. Hay asserts that we create every illness in our body out of our own self-criticism, resentment, and guilt.

For example, someone who believes that she is not worthy enough, or good enough or smart enough or "enough" in gen-eral will develop a physical condition that mirrors that belief. One of the most common conditions for people who feel that they are not enough is addiction. If you're concerned that you're not enough, you hoard what you have and lose sight of any moderation. For example, in food addicts this manifests as obesity—they are trying to be sure that they have enough food, an external resource, to assuage their fear that they don't have enough love, ability, insight, intelligence, or other inter-nal resource.

At the end of her book, Hay has something she calls The List, which is a list of most illnesses, common and not-so-common, and the thought pattern that is probably the cause behind them. She includes an affirmation that helps to replace the neg-

_____

* Louise L. Hay, *You Can Heal Your Life* (Carlsbad, CA: Hay House, 1987).

ative thoughts with a positive pattern. For cancer, she lists the probable cause as "deep hurt; longstanding resentment; deep secret or grief eating away at the self; carrying hatreds; feeling 'what's the use?'" She suggests patients replace these negative thoughts with a new pattern. Her affirmation is, "I lovingly forgive and release all of the past. I choose to fill my world with joy. I love and approve of myself."*

In addition to her entry on cancer, Hay also has probable negative thought patterns for related issues, such as breast problems, heart disease, back pain, and a separate entry for Hodgkin's lymphoma. If we read all the entries associated with a particular condition, they provide clues to the emotions we've been hiding, even subconsciously. In my case, her analysis of Hodgkin's lymphoma was particularly relevant. I've told you enough about my situation that you can relate to the persona I created. I was constantly trying to prove my worthiness and was afraid people would think I wasn't good enough. I went to extraordinary lengths to be "perfect," and I was exhausted. Imagine my shock when I first read Hay's entry for Hodgkin's lymphoma almost three years after I was in remission: "Blame and tremendous fear of not being good enough. A frantic race to prove one's self until the blood has no substance left to support itself. The joy of life is forgotten in the race for acceptance."** The description fit me perfectly—the only thing missing was my picture.

It's important to identify our hidden emotions because they dictate the choices we make. We shop when we don't have the

---

* Ibid., 185.

** Ibid., 198.

money and go into debt to try to prove we're enough. We have affairs or are promiscuous to try to validate our worth in our gender role, or enter codependent relationships and expect the other person to prove that we're enough. We develop physical ailments to provide an excuse for not performing. The choices you've made to avoid dealing with your hidden emotions have, in all likelihood, led to the current adversity you're facing.

One of the most obvious areas where our hidden emotions play out is in relationships. If we have not yet healed emotional patterns from childhood that started with our parents and siblings, we continue to find relationships for practice. Katrina* was abandoned by her father at a very early age. Her mother was largely absent from her life, since she had to work to support Katrina and her brother. When she was in high school, Katrina got pregnant, married the father, and had her first child when she was eighteen. Her husband immediately started cheating on her, and she did nothing, at first. For her, this was the path of least resistance. It was a familiar pattern and felt comfortable. Whenever he would apologize and come back to her, she got a rush of emotion for having avoided the abandonment again. However, the pattern repeated itself over and over until she finally realized that she had to end the marriage. But before she could ask for a divorce, her husband left her for another woman and moved to a different state, leaving her alone to raise her child.

Being so young, Katrina did not take the time to examine what this cosmic 2x4 was trying to tell her. She met another man, got married, and immediately got pregnant with her sec-

---

* The person and story are real, but the name has been changed to protect privacy. Story used with permission.

ond child. This marriage ended when he beat her so badly she landed in the hospital. After leaving him, now with two young children to raise on her own, she swore off men for years. Issues of worthiness and deservingness haunted her, but she put her focus on raising her two boys and finding a way to support them. She took low-level jobs that made just enough for her to get by.

Finally, Katrina realized that she wanted something more out of life and was presented with an opportunity to move into a career, which led her to identify some of her beliefs about what she deserved and what she could accept. Instead of taking the path of least resistance, which would have been to turn down the new job and stay in her safe position with less responsibility and less pay, she faced her fears and applied for the new job. Much to her surprise, she was hired! At about the same time, she met a wonderful man. They started as friends, but soon began to date. Fearful that she would repeat her old patterns, however, she put the brakes on the relationship for over a year, until she could be sure that she wouldn't do just what she'd done in every other relationship. She began to examine her feelings about men, her fear of being abandoned, and drew parallels between these things and the relationships she'd had in the past. Finally she decided to take a risk, and resumed dating the new man. After several years, they moved in together and eventually got married. She is currently living happily in her new job with her new husband, but first she had to examine the old emotions that were holding her back and let them go.

So how do you identify the benefit of a bad relationship, a health challenge, or a financial setback? You must be willing to look for your hidden emotions—emotions that have been hidden because they are painful. Now you have a compelling reason to uncover and heal the pain. What benefit are you getting from the situation? Answering this question will take some metaphorical thinking. Meditation will also help reveal the answers, and the meditation at the end of this chapter is geared toward identifying the benefits.

What Are You Avoiding?

What fear, anger, or resentment has lodged itself into your psyche? You know. You may not be willing to look at it on a conscious level, but rest assured that your subconscious knows what it is and why you're unwilling to face it. And it knows the benefit that your adversity can bring. Your current condition gives you an opportunity to get very clear on the emotions that have been playing out behind the scenes. You've been flying on emotional autopilot for most of your life. This has allowed you to avoid your feelings. The energy it has taken to avoid these feelings, however, has caused resistance that is now coming out in inappropriate ways. Something had to give. In order to have success in every area, you must heal the emotional wound you've been trying to avoid.

We humans fear our negative emotions. We go to such lengths to avoid them that we do ourselves great harm in the process. Usually the fear of the emotion is so strong that we actually cause ourselves more pain and suffering than we would have experienced had we just faced it. Have you ever had a splinter in your hand? You know that it's going to hurt when you pull it out, but you also know that if you don't remove it, you will get an infection, it will fester, and the whole thing will be much worse. So you grit your teeth, close your eyes, and remove the splinter.

The emotions you've been avoiding are just like the splinter, except that you haven't yet come to the realization that they need to come out. You know that going through the fear, anger, sadness, and pain is going to hurt, but you haven't yet made the intellectual connection that if you don't, your life will continue to deteriorate. Somehow you believe that you can live with this emotional splinter indefinitely, and that there will be no consequences. Now, however, it has festered and caused you to be in a painful situation. You must pull this emotional splinter out. We'll talk more about how to release emotions in the next step, but for now, you must be willing to face the things you've been avoiding.

By now, you probably have a pretty good idea of where to look for the feelings you've been avoiding. Most of us know what we really want, we're just afraid to ask for it. For that reason, most of us have an idea of the benefit we get from adversity. The greatest benefit is that you understand the urgency of finding out what you're really feeling! Also, you are getting things you were afraid to ask for otherwise. You may be getting attention, rest, help around the house, time off from a job you hate, or acknowledgment that had been denied you as a child. By identifying your hidden emotions and figuring out what you've been avoiding, you can begin to understand the benefit you are getting.

Have the Courage to Demand to Feel Good!

Facing a major life challenge takes courage in many areas, but perhaps no area is more important than asking for what we want. It is because we fail to ask for what we want that we get in this situation in the first place. However, you now have the opportunity to learn how to get what you need without having to suffer. Psychologists use the term "passive aggressive" to describe the behavior of people who won't ask for what they want but expect others to give it to them anyway. Have you been passive aggressive? If you haven't been asking for what you need and then are angry that others aren't providing it for you, chances are this term applies to you.

Many of us are passive aggressive by default. We never learned how to ask for what we wanted, or we learned that we got in trouble when we did. If your parents were busy and wrapped up in their own lives, they probably got angry with you for expressing your needs. You're a grown-up now, though, and it's time to give yourself permission to ask for what you want. It's not only the best way to have your needs met, it is also imperative that you do it to maintain your well-being.

For many of us, asking is difficult. We would rather suffer the pain and ongoing discomfort of not having our needs met than ask for what we want. The underlying issue is usually worthiness. We don't feel worthy of getting what we want. We've probably been told by our parents, teachers, and religious leaders that we are meant to suffer, and that having our needs met is somehow selfish or lazy. That is simply not the truth. We have been put on this earth to experience and express well-being. We each have unique talents to explore. The reason we manifest challenges is that we have been afraid to fully express our talents, desires, and gifts. In short, we've been conditioned to be afraid of who we are.

There's a wonderful passage by author Marianne Williamson that is frequently and incorrectly attributed to Nelson Mandela. Perhaps you've heard it:

Our deepest fear is not that we are inadequate. Our deepest fear is that we are powerful beyond measure. It is our light, not our darkness, that most frightens us. We ask ourselves, 'Who am I to be brilliant, gorgeous, talented, fabulous?' Actually, who are you not to be? You are a child of God. Your playing small doesn't serve the world. There's nothing enlightened about shrinking so that other people won't feel insecure around you. We are all meant to shine, as children do. We were born to make manifest the glory of God that is within us. It's not just in some of us; it's in everyone. And as we let our own light shine, we unconsciously give other people permission to do the same. As we're liberated from our own fear, our presence automatically liberates others.*

This quote speaks to the issue of worthiness. In order to identify the benefit you're getting, you must allow yourself to believe you deserve to have your Good. You must overcome your fear of who you really are and step forward to accept all the beauty and grace that is within you.

One way to feel good is to meditate. By getting in touch with the silent presence within, we can release tension and worry and begin to feel the presence of a higher power, something greater than ourselves. Another way to feel worthy is to sur-

---

* Marianne Williamson, *A Return to Love: Reflections on the Principles of a Course in Miracles* (New York: HarperPerennial, 1993),190-91.

round yourself with friends who see your value. There are also self-esteem books and workshops available. The important thing is to embrace good feelings about yourself.

I understand that this takes courage. Anytime we go against the things we've accepted as truth, it takes a deep re-evaluation of who we are. This introspection is certainly not comfortable, and as we've discussed in previous steps, most of us do whatever we can to stay comfortable.

The greatest benefit of your current situation is that it gives you the opportunity to stop accepting less than you truly deserve! Here you have the chance to demand to feel good, and you have an excellent excuse to do it. I doubt that any of the critics in your life will deem you selfish for wanting to resolve your current situation. It is your new excuse! Rather than feeling guilty for asking for what you want, just remember that you deserve to be successful. If you're not fully expressing your good, you're actually going against the natural order of the universe. Hopefully, this knowledge helps to take away any guilt you might feel.

Find a New Way

The good news about facing adversity is that once you identify the benefit that it brings to you, you can figure out other ways to get that same benefit without the suffering. What is it that you've been afraid to ask for? More affection from your spouse? More time off? A raise? A new job? More fulfilling friendships? What benefit are you getting from the current challenge? Answer that question, and you can figure out new, healthier ways to get the same things.

When I had cancer, I desperately needed to take care of myself emotionally. I felt guilty telling anyone no, as if it were up to me personally to make everything better for everyone else. Conversely, I was waiting for someone else to take care of me. The benefit of my cancer was to give me a break and teach me to take care of myself. Now I am much more careful about how I spend my time. I still struggle with overextending myself, but in general, I'm more balanced than I used to be. Finally, after all these years, I can relax without feeling guilty, take a day off without feeling like I'm letting anyone down, and I can be honest about my own needs and boundaries.

In another example, I had a business fail that left me in a fairly dire financial situation. All the time I had the business, I knew I wasn't fulfilling my life's purpose, but I was afraid to step outside my comfort zone and take a risk to get a new job. I was taking the path of least resistance, to just stay where I was and not have to face the rejection inherent in job hunting. Then the economy declined, and my business failed, and I was forced to get a job. In doing so, I had to face a lot of fears and insecurities, but I ended up with a job that was perfect! It was in greater alignment with my life's purpose and fit me much better. I learned to focus on my talents and ended up happier than I'd ever been.

What can you do to make yourself feel valuable? Perhaps there's something you haven't done in ages that will make you feel good again. Maybe you want to take an art class, go to the spa, or hike the Grand Canyon. Maybe you need a weekend away from the kids. Maybe you need a weekend away from your spouse! Whatever it is, allow yourself to do it—and do it on an ongoing basis.

Life is meant to be joyous. Adversity gives you a do-over. One benefit is the opportunity to make your life great, but you can't just sit in your living room and wait for the greatness to come to you. Decide to feel successful today, then think of activities that will reinforce that feeling. Right after I finished my chemotherapy, my husband took me to a spa in Santa Fe, New Mexico. We sat in the hot tubs, got a massage, had a salt scrub, and did a heat wrap (which was a new and interesting experience). My husband commented that he had never spent that much money in one day before in his life. In the grand scheme of things, that money was nothing compared to my health. After that day, I felt like I had reclaimed my body. Since then, I have realized that the benefit of my cancer was the permission to nurture myself. What benefit are you getting? How can you get it in a supportive way?

Step 3 Worksheet

1. In what way does your current situation provide you with a path of least resistance? What are you able to ask for, receive, or enjoy now that you couldn't before?

2. Rewrite your childhood. Write your childhood exactly as you would like it to have been. In a perfect world, what would your parents have been like? How would they have treated you? What was your room like? Your friends? Write the scenario you wish you had lived. Write it as if you were writing your memoirs. Keep it close and reread it whenever you start to feel angry or depressed.

3. Get a copy of Louise Hay's book *You Can Heal Your Life* from your local library or bookstore. Even if your current adver-

sity isn't physical, read the text, then look up the issues you have had over the years with your body and your health. What benefit have you gotten by resolving emotional issues with your body?

4. Get your journal and write about the emotions you are hiding. Allow yourself plenty of time to do this exercise. Be as honest as you can with yourself. You may not be aware of all the junk you have stored up, and that's okay. Just write whatever comes to your mind. As you move forward on the path to wellness, more hidden emotions will come up, and you can deal with them when they rise to your consciousness. For now, just write out any thoughts that come to mind.

5. Looking at the emotions revealed above, ask yourself, "What benefit do I get from hiding these emotions?" Does hiding them make you feel safe? Does it keep you from having to step outside your comfort zone? How is your current situation an outgrowth of your hidden emotions?

6. Once you've identified the benefits you're getting, brainstorm as many other ways as you can to get those benefits. List at least ten alternative ways for each benefit you've identified.

7. Make it your goal this week to do at least one of the activities that you listed above. Schedule the activity into your day planner, tell your family you're not available, and do whatever it takes to keep the promise to yourself that you will do something for *you* this week. If you're feeling really energized, schedule a few more of the activities over the next few weeks!

Meditation—Shadow Self

Lie down on a bed, couch, or the floor. Take a few deep breaths and fully relax your body. Begin at the top of your head, and imagine a cone of healing light slowly descending over your body. As the light touches each part of your body, that part instantly relaxes. Be conscious of the light beginning at the crown of your head, continuing over your face, neck, and shoulders. Feel all these parts relax.

(Pause)

Notice the light continuing over your chest, rib cage, stomach, arms, waist, and hips. Feel your entire core get very heavy. Then feel the light continue over your hips, thighs, knees, calves, ankles, and feet. Breathe deeply as you feel the relaxation seep into every cell of your body, even your bones. Get heavy as you relax into the surface you're lying on.

(Pause)

Now imagine that your shadow is lying right on top of you, facing you in a mirror image. This shadow has no weight or physical substance but reflects your subconscious mind. It is there with you now, facing you, gently floating above you. Imagine yourself feeling the presence of this shadow self. This self represents all the thoughts and feelings that you carry with you unconsciously. The shadow self is part of you, and as such, is willing and excited to help you. The shadow will tell you anything you want to know. Feel yourself making a connection with this self now.

(Pause)

Once you feel the connection, ask the shadow self what benefit you're getting from the challenging situations in your life. Ask silently what the lesson is that you need to learn from this, and what you have been hiding that the shadow self is trying to bring to the conscious mind. After you've asked, lie quietly and listen. If you fall asleep that's okay—just prepare yourself to remember any dreams you have. Remain with your shadow self until you feel that you have the answers you want.

(Pause)

Once you feel like your shadow has given you insight from your subconscious, ask it what you can do to get the benefit you want from another source. Ask for specific instructions that will help your body and your emotions heal so that the challenge will be resolved and you can be restored to wholeness. Listen patiently for the reply.

(Pause)

When you feel as if you're complete with the process and you have all the information you need, thank your shadow for bringing all its wisdom to you today. Imagine the shadow flipping over so that is no longer a mirror image, but rather is the exact image of you floating an inch or two above you. Now feel the shadow of the subconscious sink back into your body. You should feel a melting sensation or a feeling of increased mass.

(Pause)

Once you have reintegrated your subconscious shadow into your body, remain still for a minute or two as you evaluate the information you received. Allow yourself to be open to the things you have heard, and release any judgments that the information may have invoked. Remember that you are getting this information now because you are ready to hear it, so don't be angry or upset that you didn't have it sooner. Forgive yourself and accept the information with gratitude.

(Pause)

Take one last deep breath and bring your awareness back to the room.

You may want to have your journal handy for this exercise, and write down any insights you feel you got from your subconscious shadow. Do this meditation as many times as necessary until you feel that you truly understand the process and the message you're receiving.

Release Limiting Beliefs

*God grant me the serenity to accept the things
I cannot change, courage to change the things I can,
and the wisdom to know the difference.*
—Reinhold Niebuhr

I n the previous step, we learned that finding the benefit meant uncovering our limiting perceptions and hidden emotions. Now it's time to let them go. I know this can be frustrating. After all, how can you address them when, by the very definition I keep giving, they're *hidden*? But finding and releasing limiting beliefs is a crucial component to claiming the power in your life. Once we know we can drop the baggage, we're free to travel into our new, magnificent experience.

What's Limiting You?

What are your limiting beliefs, and where did they come from in the first place? If you're like most people, you have strong beliefs about what you can be, do, or have. Our parents, bless them, prepared us for the worst. In trying to save us from disappointment, many of them killed our dreams. Children generally know why they came to this earth. As kids, we had strong feelings about what we wanted to be when we grew up. By the time we actually grew up, however, our parents, teachers, or perhaps society in general taught us that these desires were unrealistic and placed limits on our expectations.

When you were a kid, what did you want to do when you grew up? Are you doing it? I'll wager that the vast majority of people reading this book are not. We were taught that our dreams were impractical, that doom and gloom awaited us if we followed certain paths. We learned that we couldn't make a living, that only a very few people succeed, that we were destined to fail, so it's best to let go of our dreams, plant our feet on the ground, get our heads out of the clouds, and find a profession that pays the bills. This was certainly my experience. When I was about ten years old, I was riding in the backseat of our car on the way to our cabin in the mountains outside of Denver. I remember looking out the window at the pine trees and the ruins of old gold mines and saying to my parents, "When I grow up, I'm going to be a writer. I want to live in the mountains with two horses and some dogs, and I'm going to write novels." The next five minutes changed my life irrevocably. After their laughter subsided, my parents informed me that I couldn't be a writer. They told me that there was no way I could make it, that everyone wants to be a writer but hardly anyone is good enough to actually succeed, and that I certainly wouldn't be able to make a living. I believed them. I spent the next thirty years looking for a career that would pay the bills within the limitations they set.

Throughout my twenties and early thirties, however, I couldn't quite find a career that fit. It's no coincidence that I got cancer during this time of searching. I had a limiting belief about my talents, desires, and abilities. I felt trapped by a need to make a living and hopeless about being able to fulfill my desires. The perfectionism that drove me to sickness came from these limiting beliefs. I hoped that if I did well enough in a career, I would learn to like it. I thought being perfect was my ticket to success and happiness. But that wasn't really true. It was just a deeply ingrained belief that dated back to that conversation with my parents in the car when I was ten. I'd structured my whole life around the idea that it was impossible to make a living as a writer. Once I was ready to release that belief, however, I found all sorts of people making their living as writers. I also recognized that I was already an author. At the time, I'd written my first book, which was about to be published.

What does this have to do with adversity? It shows that our deeply held beliefs aren't necessarily the truth of us. Many of the choices we make lead us away from our Good because we are trying to fit into the constricting parameters set by others. If we are able to release these limiting beliefs and replace them with a higher truth, we bring ourselves into alignment with the universe. When that happens, we are happy, content, enthusiastic, and healthy. It is easy to feel gratitude and joy. When we are in that state of being, we experience well-being, prosperity, love, and focus, regardless of our situation.

Sometimes, however, it's hard to ascertain which beliefs are limiting and which are true. The first thing you need to know is YOU HAVE NO LIMITS! You are pure energy, which has limitless potential. The only things that limit you are the boundaries you place on yourself. Second, the way to find your limiting beliefs is to make the connection between what you are thinking and how you feel.

How Your Beliefs Make You Feel

Even though we've already covered this, it's worth mentioning again because to most of us, this is a foreign concept. We aren't used to linking our thoughts and emotions. We humans live very much in our intellect, and deny or disregard our emotions. In previous steps, we talked about how disconnecting from our emotions can be detrimental to our overall success, because this disconnection keeps us isolated from our inner wisdom. Limiting beliefs drag us down the emotional scale, while beliefs that reinforce our potential lift us up. In order to identify and release limiting beliefs, we have to recognize how they make us feel.

When you think any thought, you automatically have an emotional reaction to that thought. Sometimes your emotional reaction is mild because the thought doesn't evoke a strong feeling, and sometimes the reaction is quite intense. For example, think "The grass is purple." What kind of emotional reaction did you have? It probably wasn't very intense. You might have felt irritation or annoyance that someone was making such an outlandish statement, or you might have been amused at the thought. But regardless of your emotional reaction, it probably didn't push any buttons. Now think, "I'm lazy and won't amount to anything." You probably had a much different emotional reaction.

Emotional reactions are programmed into us along with the beliefs that evoke them. If you grew up hearing criticism, you probably have a violently negative emotional reaction when you hear it now, no matter how much evidence you have that it's not true. Every time you think a hurtful thought or hear a negative phrase, a lifetime's worth of pain and fear come with it. If someone you cared about, especially a parent, originally told you that you were lazy, for example, you probably have some subconscious fear that they are correct. Perhaps much of what you've accomplished in life has been an unconscious effort to prove that person wrong. This programming is deep and long-standing, and it takes a high level of self-awareness to change it.

Once again, let's go back to the Law of Attraction, which states that we attract to us exactly what we focus on with strong emotion, whether we do it consciously or not. If you've been subconsciously carrying the belief that "I'm lazy and will never amount to anything," and if that belief carries an emotional charge, the Law of Attraction will bring to you circumstances and events that reinforce that belief and make it more true for you as time goes on. It will seem to be objective proof that you will never amount to anything, when in reality the universe is just bringing you experiences that support your belief.

The good news is that beliefs can be changed, and fairly easily, too. The thought "I'm lazy and will never amount to much" is a thought—nothing more. It lives only inside your mind, planted there when you were too young to know better. Because it causes such an intense emotional reaction, you have been reinforcing it your entire life through the Law of

Attraction. Now you can replace that belief with another belief that makes you feel better by identifying where you are on the emotional scale, and looking for the better-feeling thought. Perhaps you can't get all the way to "I'm industrious and worthy of great success" in one jump. That's okay. Start with a thought that evokes a more positive emotion, such as "I have good balance in my life between work and rest." Focus on that thought until it becomes the new truth for you.

How long will it take to replace a negative thought? There's no easy answer to that question. As far as the universe is concerned, it takes no time at all. As soon as you start to think the more positive thought, you send out better vibrations and begin to attract events to you that correspond to those improved vibrations. If you have habituated a thought pattern over many years, however, it becomes more difficult to change. It also depends on how much time you spend policing your thoughts and how much commitment you have to it. If you think the new, positive affirmation once or twice and then forget about it, you probably aren't going to experience very quick or effective results. If, however, you write the new belief on an index card, or maybe several, and keep them posted around your home, your office, in your wallet, and on the dashboard of your car, you're going to experience results more quickly. Also, recognize and be grateful for *any* positive results, no matter how small. Noticing all your wins will also accelerate the process.

It can be frightening to identify how thoughts make you feel. You must remember that you are safe with all your feelings. Don't try to avoid the negative feelings—that's how they stay hidden. If you make it your goal to never feel fear, anger, sadness, or any emotional pain, you are never going to be able to be honest with yourself about how you're feeling, and therefore you won't be able to improve your thoughts and vibration. Over time, you will also lose the ability to feel joy, love, pleasure, and peace, as you disconnect completely from emotions. One of the great myths of the self-help movement is that you should never have a negative thought. That causes a lot of damage, as we saw in Step 1, because when we deny our negative feelings, what we resist, persists.

As you begin to practice understanding how thoughts make you feel, don't worry about where the belief originally came from and try not to judge yourself for having it. Don't focus on being angry with whoever put the belief in your head, or with yourself for believing it. Just uncover the core belief and identify the feeling behind it. Then look to your environment to find whatever proof you can of the opposite of that belief. To go back to our earlier example, if your belief is that "I'm lazy and will never amount to much," look at the successes in your life. Make a list of the wins that you've gathered. Have you recently received a raise at work? A promotion? Have you created a new household budget or gotten the kids to all their appointments on time? No win is too small to be included on the list.

As you make your list of wins, really relish the way they make you feel. Take plenty of time to bask in the feelings of accomplishment, pride, and power. Don't dismiss any win as too small or unworthy of your attention. Even just getting enough sleep at night or showing up on time for a doctor's appointment can be considered a win toward taking proper care of yourself. We have such a tendency to focus on what we do wrong, and those things make us feel bad. The point of recognizing your wins is to highlight how many things you accomplish in a day that you completely ignore. Focusing on small wins quickly leads to bigger and bigger ones.

Another effective tool for tuning in to how your thoughts make you feel is to get still at least once an hour and ask yourself what you're feeling in that moment. Regardless of what the feeling is, be sure that you take the time to feel it. If you know you have to feel something for only a minute or two, it's easier to face any unpleasant emotion. One of the goals here is to break the habituated pattern by periodically taking your mind off autopilot, tuning in to how you feel, and concentrating on feeling better. The more you do this, the more you will be able to uncover and shift the thoughts that evoke the negative feelings.

I suggest you practice changing your thoughts with a fairly simple, neutral thought first. Don't jump into the big ones. Try something that you have already almost completely transformed, and work on transforming it the rest of the way. When I first started doing this work, I focused on my beliefs about my body. It seemed like a good place to start, since I'd been obsessed with losing weight since I was five. After I had cancer, I decided to stop doing battle with my body over how much it weighed and start appreciating it for being healthy and alive. It also helped that over the course of the previous ten years I had slowly lost almost fifteen pounds. I started to replace the belief that "I'm fat and there's nothing I can do about it" with the thought "I have a healthy body that is the perfect size." The thought felt hopeful and empowering. The results were *amazing*. With almost no effort, I dropped another ten pounds and was in better shape than I had ever been in my life.

As you take time each day to *feel*, you get better at identifying the thoughts behind the feelings and finding thoughts that make you feel just a little better. Once you're doing this on a regular basis, you will begin to have access to your subconscious world that has been hidden from you for years. As you begin to see into your subconscious more easily, you'll be able to answer the question at the root of all success: What do you really want?

What Do You Really Want?

What flashed into your head when you read this heading? I know that something came to your mind, and you probably dismissed it before it ever had a chance to take hold in your consciousness. We all know what we want from life, but like most of our feelings, we've buried it for years. You may think you already have what you want, but I'm here to tell you that you wouldn't be facing a challenge in any area of your life if you were living your dreams. You may have a life that *should* be a dream life, but you wouldn't have met the cosmic 2x4 if you were happy with it. You may have a nagging feeling that something's not right, or you may be in complete denial. Your lack of understanding is merely an illusion—a trick your subconscious plays on you to keep you from feeling disappointment, shame, or anger. No matter how confused you may feel about what you want from life, deep inside you know the answer.

Most likely, you had a dream when you were younger, just like the one I shared earlier, but you probably were told that your dream was impossible, so you abandoned it. Yet something within you still yearns for that dream. That yearning is causing confusion within you. On a subconscious level, you know what you want, but your conscious mind keeps telling you it's impossible. Because of this internal conflict, you feel trapped, helpless, and hopeless in a life that looks like it should work but somehow doesn't quite fit you. Think of an article of clothing. On the hanger, there's nothing wrong with the piece—no outward tears, stains, or flaws. But when you put it on, it just doesn't fit right and isn't very comfortable. If you've been living a life that isn't the life of your dreams, you're wearing clothes that don't fit.

In order to release your limiting beliefs, you have to figure out what you want. To do this, you must use your imagination and keep an open mind. The worksheet and meditation at the end of this chapter are geared toward helping you identify what you want. All you need is the courage to look at your dreams and passions and make a commitment to move toward them. You don't need to make a radical shift all at once. In fact, I would urge against taking any drastic steps at this point. But once you identify what you want, you can begin moving toward it in small, safe ways that give you hope for a better situation without instilling fear of losing your health and security.

One easy exercise you can do to figure out what you really want is to get a small notebook and place it next to your bed. Every morning when you first wake up—before you get out of bed or brush your teeth or use the bathroom—ask yourself what you would do that day if you were completely independent. If money were no object, and you didn't have to work or care for children or parents, or meet any of your other obligations, what would you spend that day doing? Write your answer in the notebook and flip to the next clean page. Do this every morning for thirty days, and don't look back in the notebook until the end of the thirty days. Some of the entries may be outlandish (I had one that said "fly to Paris for lunch"), but taken as a whole, you'll get a very clear idea of how you want to spend your life.

Janet* provides a great example of someone who found what she wanted and released her limiting beliefs. As a youth, she was an athlete who excelled at track and field events. She was so good in high school that her coach suggested that she call an Olympic trainer and investigate the possibility of competing on the US Olympic team. This was Janet's dream, but when she talked to her parents, they discouraged her. It was the 1970s, and they didn't feel that it was proper for a young woman to be a good athlete. Her parents were afraid that she might be "turned into" a lesbian if she were too athletic, and men might not find her attractive if she were too strong. So she gave up her desire to compete in the Olympics, but she did receive a track scholarship to college. Because of the financial assistance, her parents were delighted to have her on the university team, but they made it clear that her athletic talents were a means to an end.

Janet got her degree in marketing and quickly got a job after college. She still jogged daily, but otherwise was no longer involved in track and field. Soon she met a nice man, got married, and eventually had three daughters. The little girls played soccer and other sports along with their classmates, and Janet encouraged her daughters' athletic abilities. Then when her oldest daughter was in high school, the track coach suggested

---

* The person and story are real, but the name has been changed to protect privacy. Story used with permission.

that they look into the possibility of her training with an Olympic coach. On the surface, Janet was overjoyed and supportive, knowing that her daughter had a once-in-a-lifetime chance to go for the gold. Janet and her husband called the trainer without delay.

Then about three months after their daughter started working with the Olympic trainer, Janet was diagnosed with breast cancer. It was unusual, since breast cancer did not run in Janet's family and she was fit and healthy otherwise. Still, the doctor did a lumpectomy and started Janet on chemotherapy. Throughout her treatment, Janet continued to go to her daughter's track and field events, and to support her second daughter as she excelled at lacrosse.

Despite the fact that her daughters were living *her* dream, she couldn't quite feel supportive on an emotional level. At first she thought she was just distracted by the cancer, but after six months she was in remission, and she still felt conflicted about attending her oldest daughter's track events. One year later, the doctors found a lump in her other breast. She had another lumpectomy, started more chemo, and immediately went to see a therapist. Something instinctively told her that there was a psychological reason for her recurrence of cancer and that it was linked to her ambivalence about her daughter's athletic success.

After working with the psychologist for eight weeks, Janet had an epiphany—she realized she had a deeply ingrained belief that women should not be athletes. Although on a conscious level she felt she was being a good mother by encouraging her daughters, she also had a limiting belief that told her she was endangering her daughters' futures by allowing them to pursue athletic careers. She was conflicted by the programming she'd received from her parents, and although her intellect told her that she was doing the right thing, the deeper, limiting belief made her feel guilty and ashamed that she was putting her kids at risk of lonely, miserable futures. Her outdated belief that an athletic woman was destined to wind up old and alone was so strong that she couldn't release it without psychological help.

After working with the therapist, Janet got up the courage to talk to her parents about her own past. When she sat down with them and explained her fears for her own daughters, her mother said, "Oh, honey—times have changed! Of course you want your daughter to be an athlete! Never squelch a budding talent." Janet was furious, but after a few months and a lot more sessions with the therapist, she was able to forgive her mother's change of heart, and even find some humor in it. Finally, after a few more months of therapy, Janet could let go of the limiting belief about women in athletics and feel true joy while watching her daughters compete.

Today Janet has been in remission for two years. Her eldest daughter is training for the Olympics, and Janet works part time as her youngest daughter's lacrosse coach. Janet is running again, and even schedules one long-distance run a month with her oldest daughter. She has started a program in her local school system to teach young women the beauty of their athletic bodies, and she is happier than she has ever been in her life—but first she had to find her limiting belief and let it go.

Learn to Appreciate Your Talents

One of our greatest limiting beliefs is that we are not worthy of happiness, joy, love, and ease. Once again, our parents probably instilled this in us, but we really can't blame them. They learned it from their parents, and they from theirs before them. Sometimes our teachers and religious leaders also contribute to the belief. Most organized religions teach that we were born with original sin and that we have to spend the rest of our mortal lives gaining acceptance by a judgmental and punishing god. Our teachers might add to this collective consciousness of guilt as they claim to be experts in our aptitudes and capabilities. As a child, I heard over and over, "What makes you think you can _____?" (Insert anything here.) No matter what I wanted to do, someone was there to shoot me down.

What if none of this were true? What if we came to earth as perfect beings and have absolutely nothing to prove? Our souls, our subconscious being, our higher self, whatever you want to call the nonphysical part of us, came to earth to express and experience life. Metaphysically, that is the only reason that our existence makes sense. A field of energy can't experience the tangible realities of earth. Formless energy can't smell flowers, taste fresh-baked chocolate chip cookies, enjoy the smoothness of a baby's skin, hear the beauty of a symphony or appreciate the sight of a field of wildflowers in June. In order to experience any of those things, quantum energy had to take a form. We are the manifestations of that universal energy.

Consequently, just being here makes us worthy of whatever we want to express and experience. It comes down to our choice. If we want to experience guilt, unworthiness, unhappiness, fear, pain, and anger, we certainly can, merely by focusing our attention on the thoughts that evoke those emotions. If we prefer to experience joy, fulfillment, appreciation, love, and bliss, we simply focus on thoughts that conjure up those emotions in us. Our experiences aren't good or bad, they are just results. We are free to choose which experiences we have on this earth, but worthiness is not the issue.

One way to break free of feelings of unworthiness is to stay in a constant state of gratitude. We discussed gratitude in Step 1, and I can't stress how important it is to appreciate everything around you. I live in Colorado, and it is impossible for me to have a negative thought or feeling when I look up at the Rocky Mountains outside my window and thank the universe for putting them right there in my view. I feel like the luckiest person on earth to be able to have them in my backyard and to experience their beauty in every season. Indeed, I feel like the universe put the mountains there for my sole enjoyment. When I'm in that state of gratitude, I have no question of my worthiness.

Another way to feel worthy is to look at all the gifts that have been given to you. We did the gratitude journal exercise in Step 1, but I want you to look at the good things in your life from a slightly different perspective. Look at them now as gifts from a generous universe to a worthy and deserving member of the family. If you have children, realize that although genetics played a role in their creation, it was the laws of the universe that brought about their birth and blessed you with them. If you're having trouble with your children, focus on them as babies, before they may have been socialized into their own thoughts of unworthiness and despair.

Ultimately, you must evaluate and appreciate your talents. Take a look at the things for which people consistently compliment you. These talents were given to you by the universe.

Don't discount them! People used to tell me all the time that I was a good writer and had great public speaking abilities. I dismissed these compliments because I thought everyone could write and speak well. It was only after I had a business partner, a smart man with an MBA from an Ivy League school who couldn't string together three sentences and have them make sense, that I realized that I do have a unique talent. This was one small piece of evidence of my worthiness.

You are worthy of great joy and great love. The reason for your presence here on this earth is to grow and thrive. You are worthy of whatever desire you have—you wouldn't have the desire if it didn't come from a higher power. It isn't wrong to want what you want, and you are worthy of having it. Thinking you don't deserve the best is just a limiting belief.

Effective Releasing Processes

For many people, releasing limiting beliefs—and the emotional blocks attached to them—is the hardest thing to do. We have held on to our limits for so long that they feel like a part of us. Try this exercise: grab a pencil and hold it in your hand as tightly as is comfortable while you continue to read the rest of this section.

We humans have the bad habit of clinging to our emotions. Although these emotions feel like they are very much a part of us, they are merely just habits we have picked up over the years. Our brain gets wired to react to certain stimuli in certain ways, and the old emotions get evoked so many times that we feel as if it's the only way to react. As I've stated before, we have the choice of how we feel. We can choose to allow the familiar emotions to flood through us and keep us in our comfort zone, or we can take a more rational perspective and choose a thought that will make us feel differently—hopefully better. This sounds so easy, doesn't it?

Sometimes, though, you're doing your best to choose your thoughts and working all the steps in the program, but you're still not manifesting what you want. This means you have an emotional block that is keeping the limiting belief locked in place. There are several ways that you can deal with emotional blocks, some quicker and more effective than others. The most common way, a way that you may have tried, would be to go to therapy. Therapy can be beneficial in uncovering things in our past that continue to haunt us, and I highly recommend it if you have a lot of emotional baggage to unpack. Be sure you get an excellent therapist, however. Sometimes, therapists can keep you stuck by having you focus on all the things in your past that have made you unhappy. Although it is good to look at these events so that you can move through them, the goal needs to be just that—TO MOVE THROUGH THEM. Don't stay stuck in the past. Learn what you need to learn and move on. The downside to therapy is that it can take awhile to feel better, which makes sense. It took you decades to create the emotional habits you have—it will probably take you months or years to get rid of them.

If you feel as if you're pretty clear on what your blocks are, I suggest one of the two following techniques. The first is called the Emotional Freedom Technique (EFT), which you can find out more about at www.emofree.com. The idea behind EFT is that our bodies have energy meridians, and our emotions work in concert with those energy lines. These subtle energies are the basis for the fields of acupuncture, ancient Chinese medicine, and applied kinesiology. The technique itself is simple, although you will want to practice it alone at first because you may feel a bit silly doing it. I can personally attest to how powerful it is, however.

Basically, to release emotions with EFT, think of the negative situation you want to change and affirm that, although you are having this negative experience right now, you deeply and completely love and accept yourself anyway. As you affirm that, you stimulate a series of points on the energy meridians by tapping on them. As I said, you feel a little silly at first, tapping on your eyebrow and your collarbone and the top of your head, but the results are definitely worth it.

The first time I tried EFT I was home in bed with a cold and a terrible sore throat, and as I read the EFT Manual, I had a very healthy dose of skepticism. I started the tapping, however, affirming that, even though I had a sore throat, I deeply and completely loved and accepted myself anyway. As I began doing the "circuit," I could barely talk. My voice was hoarse, I was miserable, and I thought the whole thing was stupid. Halfway through my second circuit about ninety seconds later, my throat quit hurting, my voice was strong, and I was cured. It was amazing!

Although I'm a believer now, I recognize that some issues take longer than my miraculous ninety seconds to release. For example, I use EFT around issues of financial abundance, which for me are the deepest and hardest to release. It took anywhere from two to thirty days of practicing for these issues to go away. Still, that's better than years of therapy. For current challenges, you'll have a powerful idea of the emotional blocks that underlie them after doing steps 1 through 3 of this book. Focus on those emotions specifically, and EFT will provide a quick and effective way to release the emotional blocks that stand between you and boundless success.

Another effective technique for releasing emotions is the Sedona method.* Like EFT, the Sedona method is a deceptively simple way to find and let go of emotional blocks. It asks you a series of four simple questions, and as you answer them you release feelings you've stored for years. The Sedona method addresses thoughts and feelings that are at the root of whatever problem you're having and helps to resolve the problem once and for all. The premise is that we made a choice long ago to hold on to negative emotions, and now it is time to let them go. When you release the limiting emotions, the energy you free up can be put to use for other things, and your new openness will allow health, well-being, and joy to flow into your experience.

Still holding the pencil? You forgot that you were even holding it, didn't you? It started to feel like part of your hand. Now let it go. How does your hand feel? It probably feels a little strange and may still be "shaped" like it is holding the pencil. You may even have adapted your movements to accommodate the pencil without realizing it. That is the way it is with our emotions. They are not really a part of us, but we get so used to clutching them, both physically and psychologically, that we have trouble letting them go. Try one of the techniques we've discussed, and experience the freedom that follows.

----

* For more information, see Hale Dwoskin, *The Sedona Method: Your Key to Lasting Happiness, Success, Peace, and Emotional Well-Being* (Sedona, AZ: Sedona Press, 2003).

Step 4 Worksheet

1. Get a piece of paper and a pen. Sit quietly for a moment and imagine that you are graduating high school. As a graduation present, a distant relative gives you a magic lamp. When you rub the lamp, a genie pops out and offers to take you down any life path you want. How would you like to spend your days? What would bring you the most joy? Focus more on how you want to feel than on what you want to have. Don't censor yourself! As thoughts come into your mind, write them down and take as long as you need so you include everything you could possibly want. When you can't think of anything else to tell the genie, read over what you wrote. Are you spending your days doing those things? What are five small things you can do today that will move you closer to doing any one of them?

2. What are you keeping around the house that you can let go of? Clean out your closets, drawers, wallet, kitchen cabinets, and garage. Release anything that you haven't used in a year. This will allow the universe to bring more Good to you.

3. Practice a full day of letting go of judgments. If you find yourself holding a judgment about yourself or anyone else, just gently release it and realize that the situation isn't right or wrong, it just is. Don't judge yourself for judging— just notice how often during the day you view the world in this polarizing way.

4. In your journal, write down the limiting beliefs you heard about key areas of your life, such as health, relationships, and finances. Do you believe you can trust the opposite

sex? Do you expect to get sick as you age? Do you trust that you can make plenty of money? List any false belief you have, like "I'll never find the perfect mate" or "I can get ahead only by sacrificing my social life." Write these beliefs in your journal and then write "This is not the truth of me" next to each one.

5. Download the free EFT manual from www. emofree.com. Learn the basic technique and practice it for a week.

6. Go to a bookstore or library and get a copy of *The Sedona Method*. Practice answering the questions in the book and let go of any feelings that make you feel less than healthy.

7. Determine to live an unlimited life. Begin making a list of dreams that you gave up in the name of practicality or sensibility. Decide that it is time now to pursue your desires and hit a home run!

Meditation—Draining the Mind

Take a deep breath and let go. Relax your body completely, releasing anything that doesn't feel right in your physical self. Let go of any tension from your muscles, anything that gives you butterflies in your stomach, and make it a point to relax your shoulders. Take as much time as you need to be sure that your body is free of anything holding it out of alignment.

(Pause)

Imagine that your mind is a deep well. You can see the water on the surface of the well—this represents your conscious mind. Beneath the surface, however, is a deep store of water that you haven't seen or accessed in a very long time. Like any water standing for a long time, it has become stagnant, and there are places where unhealthy things are growing. Imagine the depths of the well, and anchor that picture in your mind.

(Pause)

Now you're going to drain the well. First, imagine yourself scooping out a bucket of fresh water from the surface and placing it aside. This represents the knowledge and skills you need to function in your daily life. As a percentage of everything in the well, it is relatively small. You can now get rid of everything else and still maintain any information you need. Now, imagine that there is a pipe at the bottom of the well that has been closed for years—maybe even decades. Open the valve on the pipe and allow all the water to drain out. Really imagine how this feels, and notice your mind being emptied of every conscious or unconscious thought. Remember, your necessary skills are protected in the bucket. Take some time to embody the feeling of draining the stagnant, dead thoughts from your mind.

(Pause)

When you feel like your mind is truly empty, close the drain valve and just rest in this feeling. Don't rush to fill it up or attempt to replace the old thoughts. Relax in the idea that your human mind is now a part of the Divine Mind, and that there is nothing there except the pure thoughts of Spirit.

(Pause)

Now picture pure spring water bubbling up into the bottom of the well. Now that the pressure of the stagnant water has been removed, the natural spring below can send its stream of water up into the well. This water is naturally aerated and pure, and has nothing murky in it. It is refreshing, life-giving, and constantly new. It is a never-ending supply that can't go stale or stagnant. Feel the pure, clean thoughts of power, inspiration, and faith flow into your mind. Know that you never have to hold on to thoughts that don't nourish your mind and your body. You always have access to an endless supply of healthy, pure thoughts.

(Pause)

With the feeling of purity, clarity, and refreshment filling your mind and body, begin to bring your awareness back to the room, but keep the feeling of your mind being wide open. Allow any thought that doesn't feel good to drain out of your mind on an ongoing basis, while you fill your mind with healthy, energetic thoughts. Picture yourself living every day with a clean, open mind.

STEP 5

Make a Plan for Success

*Take the first step in faith. You don't have to see
the whole staircase, just take the first step.*
—MARTIN LUTHER KING JR.

Okay, it's time for the rubber to hit the road. It's critical to work through all of the thoughts, emotions, and events that brought you to your current situation, but that take you only so far. Next, you have to do something about it. The first four steps in this program have helped you examine the mental, emotional, and spiritual basis of adversity. Now you have to make a plan to get to where you want to be—and stay there.

Success isn't something that you do once and then you're done. It's a lifelong commitment to maintaining supportive rather than destructive habits. The good news is that this shouldn't be a chore. If you're doing things the way the universe intends you to, you will be joyful all the time, and the new habits you adopt won't be things you dread, but rather things that excite you every day. If your plan for success includes anything that feels like a "have to," you need to modify the plan. Life is meant to be wonderful, not an obligation.

No One Plans to Fail, They Just Fail to Plan

Okay, admit it. There have been times that you started a new, life-changing program with the best of intentions, only to drop the ball in the follow-through and never complete the program. We've all done it. We've bought exercise equipment that turns into clothing racks, set budgets we didn't maintain, and planned vacations we never took. We fail to follow through for a variety of reasons, usually because we haven't done the mental work to change our beliefs about what we want. We haven't visualized ourselves in our new situation, and we haven't released the limiting beliefs and feelings that keep us stuck. Most of all, we usually fail because we don't have a plan in place to help us succeed.

Part of the reason we fail to plan is because we don't identify what we want. We talked about this in Step 4, but now it's time to answer the question, What do you really want? We reviewed how you'd been conditioned to deny your true desires. Now it's time to get back in touch with what you want, and plan how to get it. This part can be frightening. We have become so habituated to making excuses about why we can't have what we want that we become uncomfortable when it comes to actually planning it. The truth is that we can have anything, and we attract the object of our attention. By setting goals, we focus our attention away from the problems—the illness, the crappy marriage, the ungrateful kids, the tyrannical boss, the mind-numbing job—and toward the things we do want, which is success, fulfillment, and joy.

Setting goals entails getting very clear on what success looks like to you. It's important to look at the *things* in your life that define success, but it is crucial that you examine the feelings you associate with success. The universe has an infinite number of ways to bring you what you want, and if you are clear on the feeling you want to experience, you will be amazed and overjoyed at how lavishly it can come to you.

There's some dispute about how big to set your goals. I recommend starting with believable, achievable goals and working your way up. You can always revise your goals upward once you achieve the smaller goals, but if you start with a goal you don't believe you can reach, you won't achieve it and may become discouraged.

The primary criteria for goal setting are that they must be believable, measurable, and uncomfortable. Yes, uncomfortable—I'll explain that later. First, your goals must be believable. Because you attract to you the means necessary to achieve your goals through the Law of Attraction, it is crucial that you believe you can achieve them. Second, your goals must be measurable. Now, measurable is different from quantifiable. I don't really believe in setting an external value on your goal, but I do believe that to be effective, you have to know when you're there. One way to do that is to measure your effort. For example, if you want to be healthy, define what that means. Do you want to lose weight? Measure the days you eat right, rather than pounds lost. Want to exercise more? Set the number of days you'll go to the gym. Enjoy physical activities? Get more rest? If so, set a way to measure those things.

Finally, you want your goals to feel a little uncomfortable because if they're too comfortable, it means you are still in your comfort zone. Being a little uncomfortable means that you're stretching. Pushing yourself is the only way to achieve a meaningful goal. Remember, staying in your comfort zone means maintaining the habits and actions that contributed to your current situation. If you are truly committed to lifelong success, you need to step out of that comfort zone and expand your horizons.

We will be setting goals in four different areas—physical, emotional, mental, and spiritual. There will be some overlap, of course, but they should each be distinctive and measurable. For each area, you will apply the principles listed above—they need to be believable, measurable, and uncomfortable. Write down each of your goals, and I strongly suggest that you carry them with you wherever you go. I put mine on 3" by 5" file cards and carry them in my purse. I've gotten into the habit of reading them three times a day—when I get up in the morning, in the middle of the day, and right before I go to bed. This keeps them right in front of me, and helps me focus on the things I do want instead of the conditions I don't want.

When reviewing your goals, there are some important steps to follow. First and foremost, always word your goals in a positive way. For example, set a goal for being prosperous, rather than for *not* being broke. Write a goal to find a great job rather than to *not* have your current job. Your mind thinks only in positives, so it doesn't see the "no" in the sentence. To use an example I've already given, if I say, "Don't think about pink elephants," what picture just flashed into your mind? A pink elephant, right? But I told you NOT to think of that—still your mind sees the image, not the negation of it.

You also want to write your goals as if you have them now. If you write "Someday I will have..." your goal will always be "someday." It's crucial that you set goals as if they're happening to you *right now*. It is also effective to express gratitude for the goal, as if you have already achieved it. For example, one of my physical goals was "I am so happy and grateful now that I have a strong, healthy body."

When you express your goals in the present tense, your mind won't believe them at first. You'll play an internal ping-pong match when you read the goal. You'll state your intention, and your mind will argue against it, but it is in this process that you reshape your thinking to accept the objective. You can't achieve anything until your mind accepts it as already completed. Setting goals restructures your mind to believe you've already got what you say you want. That is the magic of goal setting.

Once you've set your intentions, visualize yourself having them completed. Most of us set a goal and nothing happens. That's because in order to achieve anything, we have to recondition our mind. The more vivid you can make your visualizations, the more easily you achieve your objectives. I've used the word "visualization," but the process is more effective if you involve *all* your senses. Imagine how you will feel, what you will smell, hear, and taste, as well as see, once you have what you want. If your goal is to learn a foreign language, see yourself perfectly understanding foreign words on a page, hear your voice speaking them, and imagine the feeling of traveling to that country and conversing with the natives. The more you get into the feeling of already having achieved the goal, the more quickly you will get there.

This works because of something in your brain called the reticular activation system. This system is like a tuning fork that tunes your mind to perceive things that match patterns in your subconscious. If you plant in your subconscious mind that you are a millionaire, your reticular activation system will make you perceive the proof that resonates with that image in your subconscious. You plant the images of your goals in your subconscious through visualization, and your mind helps you perceive people, activities, and resources that get you to your goal, things you wouldn't have seen if you hadn't been vibrating at that level.

Achieving your goals shouldn't mean a lot of hard work. Once you've set the intention and visualized yourself having it, the universe will rearrange itself to help you achieve what you want. You might have to take some action, but if you've set the proper goal, the action should feel fun and inspiring rather than like a chore or a have-to.

People frequently fail to achieve their desires because they believe it will take hard work with lots of sacrifices. It shouldn't be that way at all. Remember Emma Curtis Hopkins? There is Good for you and you *ought* to have it. She doesn't say you ought to work hard and give up lots of stuff to get it. If you've set an intention you really want, visualizing it should make you vibrate at a higher frequency, which will kick the Law of Attraction into effect and draw toward you the things that make that goal a foregone conclusion.

Let's talk about the biggest barrier to achieving goals—the *how*. We frequently give up because we don't know how we're going to achieve them. We fail to go for what we really want because our intellectual minds can't figure out a plan to get them. We decide that, because we don't know how we'll achieve the goal, it can't be done. This is faulty reasoning. If you don't know how you'll do something, all that means is that you don't know how you'll do something. It doesn't mean you can't. Don't worry about the "how." The universe will take care of "how." Your job is to decide what you want, visualize the way you will feel when you achieve it, and then let the universe bring it to you.

Motivational author and speaker Jack Canfield gives a great example of trusting the process. He uses the analogy of driving a car from New York to California at night. At any time, a driver can see only as far ahead as the headlights shine—about 200 feet. You can't see Los Angeles from New York, and you have to trust that when you get to the end of the 200 feet, the headlights will show you the next step. That is the way it is with goals. Decide what you want, and as you move toward them, the way will become obvious. If you don't start because you can't see the end, you'll never get anywhere.

Setting Physical Goals

Our first goal-setting area is physical. Setting physical goals is about having the level of health and fitness that makes you feel the very best. Now, this doesn't mean a lot of guilt over what you eat or the amount of exercise you do. Remember, the goals you set should feel like fun and play, not drudgery. For example, I used to be an avid runner. When I was married to my first husband, he and I ran 10K races and half marathons, usually one every weekend. I liked being outdoors, I liked feeling strong, and I liked the camaraderie of the races, but I didn't really like running that much. After I survived cancer I switched to power walking. I love it, and I like doing it even when I don't have to. It's about fun. If you're someone who has been hearing from doctors, spouses, and parents that you have to eat better, exercise more, lose weight, quit smoking, stop drinking, give up sugar, don't eat fast food, eat more vegetables, or any of these things, you are probably reluctant to set realistic physical goals. I want you to forget everything you've ever heard or learned about your physical body when you set your goals. Don't set one because you feel like you "should"—set only those goals that you want. Maybe you want to do stretches for fifteen minutes every day, or go for a walk in the mountains or on the beach once a week. Maybe you want to eat eggplant Parmesan every Friday night. Fine. Just make sure it feels good and promotes your ongoing wellness.

What would make you feel great physically? Write down whatever pops into your mind, being sure to concentrate on how you will feel when you achieve it. What kind of energy will you have? What activities will you do? How will you feel emotionally? Then translate the answers to those questions into a present tense, positive, believable, measurable goal. An example might be, "I am so happy and grateful that I now have a healthy body, I have all the energy I need to play with my children (grandchildren), and I am able to walk up the stairs without being out of breath." Don't put limits on your physical goals.

They can apply to more than simply diet and exercise. Sure, you can set a goal to lose weight and exercise more, but what else do you want? Run a marathon? Surf in the ocean? Learn to rock climb? Take some time to really think about the things you want your body to be able to do. Nothing is off limits to you. Perhaps you've always wanted to try bungee jumping. Now is the time to do it! Set a goal that goes something like, "I am so happy and grateful now that I have the time, energy, money and physical strength to try bungee jumping." Read it every day, and pretty soon you'll be dangling from a stretchy cord.

The most common physical goal I hear is about weight loss. Most Americans struggle with losing weight. Part of the problem is that we assume that losing weight means sacrificing the foods we love, doing a lot of boring, strenuous exercise, and being trapped in a difficult or inconvenient routine of worrying about what we eat. Set the goal you want to achieve, visualize it as already done, and then don't worry about how it will happen. If weight loss is your goal, remove the focus from the scale and put it on the feeling. How will you feel when you are at your ideal size? Don't worry as much about weighing a certain number as being a certain size.

Also, don't worry about how you're going to get there—that usually evokes dread about diets, deprivation, and exhaustion. See yourself at your ideal size, and the way to get there will appear. Know that it will be easy and natural to do this. Follow your intuition and your body's own cues about when and what to eat, and the weight will fall off. It sounds radical, but once you overcome your resistance to the idea, it works. Don't talk about "losing" weight, either. What do you do when you lose your car keys? You immediately try to find them. Think of your weight loss in terms of releasing—releasing the habits that caused overeating, as well as the weight itself.

We will be setting our actual physical goals when we do the worksheet at the end of the chapter, but for now, know that you can shape your body any way you like. Medical science and quantum physics tell us that the cells in our body die and are replicated at regular intervals, which vary depending on the type of cell. Some cells regenerate in a matter of hours, some weeks, some months. The longest any cell takes to replicate is two months, which means that you have an entirely new body every sixty days. The reason you haven't seen changes before is that your thoughts told your body to create the same cells over and over again. You may not have been conscious of it, but you directed your body to produce diseased cells, fat cells, and other unhealthy cells. Now you can direct your body to produce healthy, happy, efficient cells.

Setting Emotional Goals

Physical goals are generally the easiest types to set—after all, you can see the results. Setting emotional goals is a little more complicated because it means recognizing how we feel, and then setting goals to feel better. As we've discussed repeatedly, we've been trained to ignore how we feel. Usually, emotional goals have to do with relationships—both with ourself and with others. Our goals regarding our relationship with ourself start with healing old emotional wounds, taking better care of our body, and allowing ourselves time for fun. Sometimes this includes finding a hobby or focusing on activities that feed our soul. It also means having plenty of time to be alone, contemplate, and create.

Regarding our relationship with others, emotional goals focus on friendship, romance, and the things we want out of our interactions. Do you have as many friends as you like? Are you married? Are you *happily* married? If you answered no to these questions, you can set an emotional goal for what you want in these areas.

I learned the value of emotional goals when I had cancer. That experience, like most cosmic 2x4s, took an incredible toll on my relationships. I lost many friends who just couldn't deal with the fact that I was sick. I guess this brought up their own fears of mortality, or uncomfortable associations with loved ones who had cancer, or judgment about my situation, but some of my closest friends seemed to abandon me. Friends that I saw every day suddenly were too busy to have coffee once a week. A few of them never even acknowledged my illness. I felt alone and deserted.

I did have a few surprises. A woman I had met in my Lamaze class three years earlier brought dinner to our family every night I had chemo. A neighbor down the street started leaving fresh-baked bread for us. Teachers at my daughter's preschool offered to bring her home on the days I had doctors' appointments so my husband wouldn't have to go get her. These were incredible kindnesses, and I was truly blessed to have them, but none of them led to long-term relationships with people or did anything to repair my hurt at the relationships I'd lost.

My marriage suffered while I had cancer, as well. I was wrapped up in the emotions of having cancer and didn't have the energy or the emotional resources to support anyone else. Although my husband took all the right actions, I realized that I had been the emotional support system of the marriage, and when I could no longer fulfill that role, the marriage broke down. We remained friends, but I learned more clearly what I want from a primary romantic relationship.

My experience with cancer is typical of how relationships suffer when we face adversity. I had similar experiences when I went through my divorce and lost all my married friends.

Stories of people feeling isolated when they face financial challenges are legendary. Yet we also hear how people come together through adversity to have deeper relationships, closer friends, and a greater understanding of themselves. We do this by consciously identifying with our emotional goals.

Setting emotional goals involves managing the way you respond to your feelings. Remember in Step 1 when we talked about the difference between feelings and emotions? Feelings are the sensations that you get from your body, the feedback the physical world sends you. Emotions are the way you interpret those feelings. "E-motions" are energy in motion. To give you an example of the difference, let's look at the feeling of butterflies in the stomach. Everyone can relate to the *feeling*, but it symbolizes different *emotions* for different people. Some people associate the fluttering feeling with fear, and they get sad and depressed when they experience that sensation. Others might think of excitement and anticipation and get joyful when they experience it. The "feeling" is the same, but the "emotion" is based on our individual interpretation.

As I've claimed throughout the five steps, it is possible to monitor and control our emotions, even if we don't always understand them. I frequently feel like crying, and that used to upset me. I always tried to figure out what was wrong with me, or why I was so depressed that I needed to cry all the time, or what deeply ingrained trauma was coming back up. This emotional self-examination made me depressed and angry, so every time I felt like crying, I associated it with anger and depression. I set a goal to disassociate those emotions from the feeling of crying and whenever I wanted to cry, I would say a few quick words of gratitude for my sensitive nature and let it go. In doing that, I took all the power out of the tears. I still cry all the time, but now I'm a lot happier when I do.

Setting emotional goals means determining how you want to show up in the world. One great way to do this is to determine your emotional intelligence.* Are you a happy person? An angry one? Are you an inspiration to your friends? Or are you the one who always has a crisis? Once you determine how you want to feel, you are able to set emotional goals for yourself that reflect the way you want to live. Remember, everything is created from the inside out. Don't say you'll be happy later, when things get better. Be happy now, and success will follow.

It may help to recall the Emotional Guidance System from Jerry and Esther Hicks's book *Ask and It Is Given.* If you have the book, find your set point on the emotional scale, and then decide where you want to spend most of your time. Hopefully you will want to be in the range from contentment to love/appreciation/bliss. Once you decide where you want to be, decide what will get you there.

Although we have control over our emotions, we still must be cognizant of the feelings caused by various situations. Basically, we can choose to make our emotional lives easy or hard. For example, if being in your marriage brings up uncomfortable feelings, you can put a lot of time and energy into trying to interpret those feelings in a positive way. This is admirable and honorable if your long-term goal is to stay in the marriage at all costs, but if your emotional goal is to be happy and release resistance, you may want to remove yourself from the situation that causes the uncomfortable feelings. This could mean

---

* For more about Emotional Intelligence, see Travis Bradberry and Jean Greaves, *Emotional Intelligence 2.0* (San Diego, TalentSmart, 2009).

having a frank discussion with your spouse about things that bother you, going to marriage counseling, or even ending the marriage—it's your choice. Do you struggle to pull positive emotions out of uncomfortable feelings (which is difficult under the best of circumstances), or do you take yourself out of the situation that causes the painful feelings? It all depends on your goals.

When setting your emotional goals, keep in mind again that these things should come easily. The spiritual path to success isn't a struggle—it is a joyful thing! Set only those emotional goals that make you feel good. I hope none of us consciously sets a goal to be around people who make us mad or depressed, but sometimes we cling to relationships that do just that. Why do we do this? Because we don't want to hurt the other person, because we're afraid to be alone, because we don't think we deserve any better, because we doubt that any better relationships will come along—there are plenty of reasons. By working to stay in a relationship that doesn't make us feel happy, we are unconsciously setting a goal to stay unhappy.

As you set emotional goals, examine fear. We already talked about fear and how it creates toxic biochemicals. It also keeps us mired in toxic relationships and situations. Hate your job? Why don't you leave it? Fear. Unhappy in your marriage but won't get a divorce? Why do you stay? Fear. Depressed every time you talk to your mother? Why do you stay in contact with her? Guilt, which is fear's cousin. Facing fear head-on is something very few people are willing to do because, of course, it's scary, but uncovering these fears will help you set truly fulfilling emotional goals.

Setting Mental Goals

What are you doing to keep your mind sharp? Watching television doesn't count. In order to be successful, we must keep our minds healthy. Studies have shown that people who are avid readers, card players, and crossword puzzle aficionados are far less likely to get Alzheimer's disease or other forms of dementia than people who are not. That means that in order to stay healthy, you have to use your brain.

Is there something you've always wanted to learn? A book you've wanted to read? A course you want to take? What has been stopping you? Many people who've overcome a major challenge understand that they have been given another chance to do things differently.

Few, however, take that opportunity. One man from my cancer support workshop went back to college at age sixty-two. He was a retired stockbroker and had never finished his college degree. He got a bachelor's degree and went on to get a master's in history—simply because it was something he wanted to do. He thought it would be a good way to stay busy. He ended up writing a number of articles for the local historical society's quarterly magazine and becoming a recognized expert in historic preservation, all because he wanted to keep his mind busy.

Mental goals don't have to be as lofty as completing a college degree. Some people take up reading for enjoyment. Others decide that they want to know more about a certain topic and begin researching it on the Internet. Some go to the local community college and begin taking courses that sound like fun.

Still other people join service clubs and organizations that have monthly guest lecturers on a wide variety of topics. You can also volunteer at your local museum or library, or travel to different cultures and learn about them.

Personally, I wanted to learn German. When I was going through chemotherapy, I was in the midst of completing my PhD, so I felt like I had plenty of mental stimulation, and I certainly didn't want to have to study any more than I was already. A few years later, however, I felt the urge to speak German. My grandparents spoke it and I knew it as a child, but I hadn't spoken it since I was in college. I got out my old college textbook, my daughter gave me an "instant immersion" CD series, and I began to relearn German. It has been great fun, and one of my new goals is to take my daughter to see where our family originated in Austria.

Whatever mental goal you set, be sure it's something you really want to do, learn, or know. If your mental goal feels like homework, you'll never do it. Again, the point of goal-setting is to do the things you love, feed your soul, and give you great joy.

Setting Spiritual Goals

Since the start of the twenty-first century Americans have shifted to identifying more with the category "spiritual but not religious" than any one specific denomination. Spirituality is different from religion in that there is very little dogma to it. Religious leaders make sure that their congregants live by a stringent set of rules set forth by a church hierarchy. Spirituality, however, is about individuals getting in touch with their own soul—their uniqueness, the energy that created them.

Every major religion has a core of spirituality, stating that we are unified with our creator. In the Bible, Jesus says, "I and my father are one," and there are similar phrases in every major religious text. Quantum physics has proven that this is true, showing that the separation that exists between each person and his environment is really just an illusion—different shapes of energy that give the appearance of being separate, at a sub-atomic level are identical.

Similarly, New Thought traditions such as Religious Science, Unity, and Divine Science have seen an increase in the number of followers, even as attendance in more traditional churches has declined, and secular healers and teachers have appeared to fill a void brought by traditional religion. Authors, talk show hosts, and celebrities such as Oprah Winfrey, Jack Canfield, Wayne Dyer, Stephen Covey, Marianne Williamson, Jerry and Esther Hicks, and even Madonna are setting the stage for people to seek out a spirituality that empowers them to be more of who they are, rather than blindly follow doctrines written thousands of years ago. I joke that today people are increasingly following the "gospel according to Oprah."

What does all this mean to you? It means that, regardless of your religious upbringing and regardless of your current beliefs about God, religion, or spirituality, your soul is crying for a connection with your source. Psychologist Carl Jung called this the Transpersonal Self and believed all people are seeking to understand and unify with it. In order to find the power within, you must set goals that allow you to commune with your higher self on a daily basis. There are numerous ways to do this, and the choices you make in this area are personal and individualized.

Many people find nature to be a great spiritual inspiration. I know that I feel more connected to my source when I'm hiking in the Colorado Rockies than I ever did when I sat in church. Others find their spiritual needs fulfilled by volunteering their time to organizations that help the planet or the people on it. Still others feel the most connected when they are working with children. Some join study groups or New Thought churches and become part of a spiritual community that way. Regardless of what you do, I urge you to create a spiritual practice.

In some ways, I've already coerced you into a spiritual practice. Meditation has been recognized by every major spiritual tradition to be an excellent practice for stilling your mind and communing with your soul. If you've never meditated before, the guided meditations at the end of each chapter will help get you started. You may want to take a meditation class, or start a meditation journal where you write down any thoughts that occur to you while meditating. Studies have shown that people who meditate live longer and are healthier than people who don't. The Simontons' research showed that meditation was vital to people surviving cancer—remember, their terminal cases healed themselves using nothing other than guided meditation.

It doesn't matter what kind of spiritual practice you implement. Just do something. Get in touch with your soul every day. Take time to marvel at the beauty of nature and the humanity around you. Make sure you check in with yourself about how you are feeling and what you want from life, and continue to practice forgiveness and gratitude from Step 1. This is a magic combination that will keep you on the path to success.

A great example of someone who used her spirituality for success is Julie.* After being raised Catholic, she found New Thought while in her early twenties. She went to see some of the speakers and periodically would drop in on a Sunday service but didn't really create a spiritual practice until many years later when she found herself at a career crossroads. After going to graduate school and getting an advanced degree, she realized that she didn't like the field she was in, yet she was unwilling to go back to school to be trained in a different one now that she was over forty.

Then one night, she dreamed about being more spiritual, having a flexible lifestyle, and doing work that excited her. She couldn't see how that could happen in her current career, but she put spiritual steps into place to bring it about. She began to meditate on how it would feel to have the perfect job and what her life would be like when she made the amount of money she felt she deserved. She wrote affirmation cards about having plenty of value and loving her job. She frequently wrote in her journal about anything that frustrated or discouraged her, so that she could let it go and stay focused on her goal. Finally, she surrounded herself with positive, like-minded people who reinforced her self-worth.

After about three months, someone e-mailed a job posting to her for what looked like just another job. She ignored it, until another friend sent her the same listing. Finally, when it came into her in-box from a job-search website, she took a closer look. Despite the job title, this position perfectly fit her skills and provided her with the lifestyle and income she had always

---

* The person and story are real, but the name has been changed to protect privacy. Story used with permission.

desired. It also allowed her to exercise her creativity and spirituality by being involved in team building and relationship management. She applied for the job, and got it.

Julie didn't go back to business as usual, however. She continued her spiritual practices of meditation and journaling, even as she became comfortable in her new position. She continued to surround herself with supportive people, and continually sought new challenges in her job so that she could continue to use her creative skills. She now teaches the techniques of meditation, affirmation, and journaling to her coworkers and team members. She has set goals for herself in all aspects of her life, and those goals keep her from falling into the abyss of fear. She moves toward her goals every day and has doubled her level of responsibility and income over a five-year period.

The Rule of 5

It's great to set goals, but you have to act on them. Most of us set goals, work on them for a few days, maybe a couple of weeks, and then give up and fall back into old habits. That's because the goals seem overwhelming. That's why I said earlier that you must set achievable goals, but even at that, many people just don't know where to start. Remember when you learned to drive a car? The instructor didn't plop you behind the wheel, hand you the keys and say, "Okay, go ahead and drive." You learned step by step. That's the most effective way to move toward your goals, too.

After you set your physical, emotional, mental, and spiritual goals, pick one from each category that you want to work on first. This can be the one that seems the easiest to achieve, or the one that is most important to you, or the one that will take the least amount of time to finish. Just pick one. Then every day, do five small things that will move you closer to that goal. You may have already started this in the exercise at the end of Step 3. You don't have to achieve the goal all at once, or do anything hard. Just pick five small things, every day.

For example, one of my goals was to write a book. I had been wanting to write it since 1998, but I kept waiting until I had six months free to devote to it. Well, I was a single mother, I owned my own business, I volunteered in the community— when on earth was I going to find six months free to write a book? Of course, I didn't, and consequently the book didn't get written. Then I heard motivational speaker Jack Canfield talk about the Rule of 5, and I had an idea. What if I wrote five pages every day? I could do that—it would take only about an hour, and if I got to my desk just one hour earlier, I could write before I even answered my e-mail. The results were amazing. I finished the manuscript in less than three months, *and* I found myself more productive in other areas of my life. Rather than taking time away from running my business, writing the book motivated me to do more. I was so energized after finishing my five pages that I got cranking on work immediately and frequently finished *earlier* than I would have had I not written. It's amazing how the universe helps you when you move toward your goals.

Every day, pick five small things to do toward one of your goals and get started. Author Johann Wolfgang von Goethe wrote, "Whatever you can do or dream you can, begin it. Boldness has genius, power and magic in it." Be sure that you are realistic, but stay focused on doing them. Write them in your day planner and make them a top priority. Don't allow phone calls, e-mail, appointments, or anything else to get in the way of doing those five things. By doing that, you're sending a message to the universe that your goals are important, and the universe will respond in kind by sending you shortcuts and ways to fulfill your desires more easily. But you must make, and keep, the commitment to yourself.

Build Your Success Support Team

All successful people, whether they've gained success in the fields of business, sports, entertainment, or the arts, know the value of having a team behind them. The same is true for you. If you want to have lifelong success, you need to have a team of people supporting you in reaching your goals. The team can include family, friends, work colleagues, doctors, therapists, spiritual leaders, or professional coaches, but they don't have to be any of those things. The most important thing is that you find a group of people who support your goals and your well-being.

The biggest factor to consider as you are creating your team is that you want people who will *support* you. If your mother has never supported anything you've ever wanted to do, she probably shouldn't be on this team. If your friends tell you that you can't reach your goals, you may have to seek out some new friends to participate in this part of your life. If your spouse blocks your plans because of fear of losing you, get some marriage counseling. If your doctors look at you as if you're the walking dead, get new doctors. Be sure that everyone on your team has a great attitude and believes in your success.

This doesn't have to be a formal team, but it should consist of people whom you consider to be your network. Have some work-out friends who will keep you motivated to achieve your physical goals. If you take a yoga or Pilates class, count the instructor as one of your team members. If you walk every morning with a group of friends, they're part of your support network. If you have a standing golf date, your golf buddies are on the team. The therapist that you have been seeing for months, the teacher of the photography class you love, and your minister may all be on the team. Whoever they are, be sure that you feel good when you're around them.

It's a good idea to have at least one person from each of the four areas of your life on your team. Have someone who promotes your physical goals, someone who supports your emotional goals, someone who understands your mental goals, and a cheerleader for your spiritual goals. Once you figure out who these people are, make a list for yourself. Talk to each of them and ask them if they are willing to be part of your support network. Explain to them that they'll be doing what they're already doing, but you'd like to count them as special friends who can help you in your goal of success. I guarantee that the people you ask will be flattered.

Many of us avoid creating a network because we don't want to bother or burden other people. We feel as if we have to go it alone and be completely self-sufficient so that we don't put undo pressure on our friends, family, and acquaintances. However, most people are thrilled to be asked to help. Imagine how you would feel if a friend or acquaintance asked you to be part of their support team. If all you had to do was something that you were doing anyway, wouldn't it be nice to feel like you were contributing to someone else's success? I guarantee that whoever you ask to be on your team will feel the same way.

Once you've decided who will be on your team, make sure that you set a time to check in with them on a regular basis. There is no set schedule for being in touch with your team, but you want to be accountable and have everyone know that you're doing what you've said you'd do. If you have a physical goal to run a marathon, you will want to have someone on your support team to motivate you to get your running shoes on in the morning when you feel like lounging in bed. If you have an emotional goal to reconnect with your girlfriends, be sure that you contact one of them frequently enough that you have a relationship. Use a smartphone or PDA, and make contact with your support team an integral part of each week.

Building your support team will keep you from slipping back into old patterns. Remember that once you start achieving your goals and having fun with your life, the possibility of self-sabotage gets further and further away from your consciousness and helps move you closer to your purpose. That is the point of creating a success team. Find your purpose and live from that place every day. Let go of worry and surround yourself with people who keep your attention focused on the joyous, fulfilling life you desire rather than the worries and fears of your previous life. Don't let anything stand in the way of finding and living your purpose, and you will be guaranteed lifelong success.

Follow Your Bliss

I'd like to add a final word here about choices. Keep in mind as you make your plan for lifelong success that you have a choice every minute of every day. You have the ability to choose your thoughts, emotions, and actions. Most of us don't make our choices consciously. We react in a series of conditioned ways, which means that we attract the same conditions we've always had. In order to succeed, you must choose your thoughts moment to moment, and choose them based on how they feel. When you are at the crossroads of emotions, choose joy.

As you find your way through adversity, you will probably notice you continue to carry a great deal of fear. After I went into remission, for the first few years everything caused fear. Because my Hodgkin's symptoms were similar to having a cold, every time I felt a cold coming on for the next three years, I was convinced that I was having a relapse. I had to really focus on wellness to keep the fear at bay. Fear is a killer. It is crucial that you stay focused on success and not let the fear get the better of you. When you feel yourself being afraid of repeating the old patterns, remember your goals, focus on your affirmations, call your support team, and choose joy.

Choosing joy is always important, even when you're not afraid. When you have too much work to do and you're nervous and stressed because you're afraid your boss will be mad and it's a beautiful day and you really want to go take a walk, choose the walk. In the larger picture, what's a little work compared to thirty or forty minutes of joy? When your kids are driving you crazy and you really want to relax but feel like you're overloaded with soccer practice and choir concerts and shuttling children everywhere, call a grandparent and go take half a day to relax and rejuvenate. When you really want to go out with a group of friends but you promised your mother you'd take her shopping for new drapes, reschedule Mom and go let your hair down. Mom will understand.

When you choose joy for yourself, you are serving everyone in your life. The more joy you have, the more energy you have. There is nothing noble about running yourself down to the point of exhaustion or being so angry and resentful that you are unpleasant to be around and have no real contribution to make. Being in a state of joy attracts more good things to you, changes your biochemistry so that you have a stronger immune system, invokes the Law of Attraction to bring your Good, and helps reinforce your new, successful habits. Get in the habit of choosing joy. It will become contagious, and the people around you will be more joyful. And you will be successful forever.

The great philosopher and scholar Joseph Campbell said, "Follow your bliss," which many of us can quote but few of us can do. We feel guilty being happy, but as we discussed in the introduction, happiness produces brain chemicals that allow you to heal, both physically and emotionally. Following your bliss means doing what you want to do and putting yourself first. It means claiming the power within you to be the creator of your life, and avoiding circumstances that don't bring you joy. By following your bliss, you can use the cosmic 2x4 to hit a home run.

Step 5 Worksheet

1. Take a few moments to get still. Then write five physical goals for yourself. Make sure these are goals you really want to achieve and that they are believable, measurable,

and uncomfortable. Maybe you want to run a 10K road race or climb a mountain. Perhaps your goals are more modest, like taking a ten-minute walk every day or stretching four mornings a week. As long as they are believable, measurable, and uncomfortable, write them down.

2. Write five emotional goals. Use the same criteria as above.

3. Write five mental goals. Use the same criteria as above.

4. Write five spiritual goals. Use the same criteria as above.

5. Find a place in your home, office, or car to post your goals. You can either post them as written statements or cut out pictures that symbolize the goals for you. Either way, put them someplace where you will be sure to see them every day.

6. Commit ten minutes every day to visualizing your goal as if you've already achieved it. Get still, relax your mind, and close your eyes. Imagine how you will feel when you've achieved your goal. Imagine how things will look, sound, feel, and smell when you have the experience of your goal. Make it as real as possible—the more real you make it; the sooner it will happen. One disclaimer—this should never feel like a chore. Expect to do this every day, but do it when you are excited to do it. The more you can get into the feeling of your goal, the better.

7. Establish your support team. Write a list of people who can help you achieve your goals. Contact them and ask if you can consider them part of your support team. Explain to them that they don't have to do anything except what they're already doing.

8. Decide upon a daily spiritual practice that will keep you connected with your source. This may be meditation, jour-

naling, walking in nature, listening to a symphony, or any number of activities. As long as it makes you feel well, purposeful, and connected, it's perfect. Begin today.

Meditation—Power Recharge

Close your eyes and rub your hands together quickly. Continue rubbing until you feel heat generated by the friction between your hands. Once you feel the heat, stop rubbing, place your hands, palms up, on your knees, and feel the energy flowing between your surroundings and your body through your hands. This energy is pure power— and it is a power that is at your disposal. Take a few minutes to feel the power surging from your hands throughout your entire body.

(Pause)

As you feel the power in the very cells of your body, take time to recognize that you have access to the infinite energy that flows through the universe. There is nothing limiting you. You have the power to be, do, or have anything you can imagine. The power pulsating through you is giving you a nudge to go forth to greater experiences. Become comfortable with the feeling of power you have.

(Pause)

While still pulsating with power, visualize your goals. See yourself achieving them effortlessly, easily. Know that the energy of the universe is moving you closer to your goals every second, and that you need not struggle or strain to get there. Everything you want is already done in the vibration of the universe, and the creative energy is pulling you toward your goals. Get excited about your goals!

(Pause)

Feel positive energy flowing through you. If you start to feel any dread, fear, or worry, bless and embrace it as an old pattern, and consciously replace it with a new thought of power and effectiveness. Forgive yourself and anyone else who might have told you that you need to struggle to achieve your goals. Feel grateful for your ability to be joyful and have goals that excite you. Bask in the feeling of gratitude for your completed goals.

(Pause)

Now, with a surge of power flowing through you, thank the universal energy for its inspiration, power, and guidance, and with great enthusiasm, open your eyes.

Conclusion

These five steps have been designed to give you a blueprint to overcoming adversity, finding your spiritual power, and living a life of fulfillment and success. Despite all appearances to the contrary, whatever adversity you've been facing has really been a great gift. By following these five steps, your life will be richer and more fulfilled than you ever thought possible. You can have better health, deeper relationships, and greater prosperity in all aspects of your life by following the steps that I've outlined, but they work only if you do them and are committed to them. A motivational speaker once said, "No one else can do your push-ups for you." To succeed, you have to focus on success. You now have a chance to live a better life than you thought possible. The choice is up to you.

Go ahead. Hit it out of the park.

CPSIA information can be obtained
at www.ICGtesting.com
Printed in the USA
JSHW021125180421
13684JS00006B/38